Praise for
Someone Could Get Hurt

"There are a lot of memoirs that are filled with sweet, syrupy stories and annoying life lessons. This is not one of them. It's an honest and hilarious potrayal of how aggravating it can be to raise a family. Even my dad would read this, and he generally thinks the name Drew is reserved for inbreds."
— Justin Halpern, author of the
New York Times bestseller *Sh*t My Dad Says*

"Drew Magary's book shows better than anything else I've read—with humor and sadness and fear and style—what it's like to be a parent. He reveals the honest terror of it. But the beauty, too, and the dragginess and joy and all the rest. If you're a parent, read it. If you want to be a parent— or know someone who does, or already is—read it. So, yeah. Just read it."
— Darin Strauss, NBCC award-winning author of
Chang & Eng and *Half a Life*

"The world needs Drew Magary's wonderfully funny, breathtakingly honest book about parenting, which reveals what few have the nerve to come right out and say: It's never going to be perfect—but there's no shortage of hilarity amid the heartaches. Parents will feel a little less alone in the company of these chapters, and nonparents will get a moving, utterly entertaining glimpse into a world that might be theirs someday. Reading this book was like being held and rocked through the joys and pains of life all night long, with no spit-up involved."
— Jen Doll, author of *Save the Date* and
senior writer at *The Atlantic Wire*

"Absolutely wonderful. Drew Magary has written an honest and funny and moving account of his journey into parenthood. He has an eye not only for the absurdities of the human condition but also for its deeper meanings."
— David Grann, author of *The Lost City of Z* and
The Devil and Sherlock Holmes

"The Father's Day book for dads who hate getting books for Father's Day. *Someone Could Get Hurt* is hilarious, unpretentious, and honest."
— Will Leitch, author of *Are We Winning?* and *God Save the Fan*

"If you know how to read, you should definitely read Magary's book. Whether you don't have children, have children, or you've recently stolen a few, you will love this."   — Joel McHale, comedian

"If you are a parent, I challenge you to not simultaneously laugh and sob through this entire book."
—Rachel Dratch, comedian and author of *Girl Walks into a Bar* . . .

"Electric prose . . . a memoir that shines with refreshing realness. For all his potty-mouthed, free-form commentary, Magary demonstrates a noble belief in love, honor, and freeze-framing moments with kids who always seem to grow up way too fast." —*Kirkus Reviews*

"Profane, touching, and hilarious all at the same time . . . straightforward and, most refreshingly, brutally honest." —*Chicago Sun-Times*

"With lineage that can be traced from Bill Cosby through Ray Romano, Paul Reiser and Louis C.K. . . . Magary provides a beautiful portrait of paternal love." —*The Plain Dealer* (Cleveland)

"Funny, profound, and above all straightforward . . . [Magary's] candor is commendable." —*Boing Boing*

COURTESY OF THE AUTHOR

Drew Magary is a correspondent for *GQ* and a columnist for Deadspin and Gawker. He's also the author of *The Postmortal* and *Men with Balls: The Professional Athlete's Handbook*. Drew has written for *Maxim*, *New York*, NPR, NBC, *Slate*, *The Atlantic*, *Bon Appétit*, *The Huffington Post*, *The Awl*, Yahoo!, ESPN, *Rolling Stone*, Comedy Central, and more. He lives in Maryland with his wife and children.

You can find more of Drew's writing at DrewMagary.com, or follow Drew on Twitter @drewmagary.

SOMEONE
COULD GET
HURT

A Memoir of
Twenty-First-Century Parenthood

DREW MAGARY

GOTHAM BOOKS

GOTHAM BOOKS
Published by the Penguin Group
Penguin Group (USA) LLC
375 Hudson Street
New York, New York 10014

USA | Canada | UK | Ireland | Australia
New Zealand | India | South Africa | China

penguin.com
A Penguin Random House Company

Previously published as a Gotham Books hardcover

First trade paperback printing, May 2014

10   9   8   7   6   5   4   3   2   1

Gotham Books and the skyscraper logo are trademarks of
Penguin Group (USA) LLC

The Library of Congress has catalogued the hardcover edition as follows:

Magary, Drew.
Someone could get hurt : a memoir of twenty-first-century
parenthood / Drew Magary.
pages cm
ISBN 978-1-592-40832-0 (HC)   978-1-592-40876-4 (PBK)
1. Parenting—Humor.   2. Fatherhood—Humor.
3. Magary, Drew—Biography.   I. Title.
PN6231.P2M34 2013
306.874—dc23
[B]
2013016261

Printed in the United States of America
Set in Janson Text · Designed by Spring Hoteling

To my brother and sister . . .

. . . and every other parent out
there still trying to figure it all out

CONTENTS

CONTENTS

A NOTE FROM THE AUTHOR

All stories contained herein are taken from memory. If you're looking for historical accuracy, I highly recommend the 1973 *Farmers' Almanac*. It's unimpeachable.

MALROTATION

We all agreed that the child must be disemboweled. The doctor stood with my wife and me in the surgical waiting room and calmly explained what he was going to do. He would make a small incision in my son's belly. He would pull out my son's small intestine and lay it out on the table, all eight some-odd feet of it. He would check to make sure that blood was flowing to every part of the bowel. Then he would untangle the tangled parts, stuff them all back into the baby's body, and hope that they stayed in place. My son, at the time, was nine days old.

Our third child was born seven weeks premature with a condition known as intestinal malrotation. The doctor explained it like this: When you're in your mom's uterus, your intestines initially form outside of your body. Then they retreat into your abdomen, twist, and your abdomen seals up around them. If you're unfortunate enough to be born with this condition (5,000-to-1 odds, though more common in premature infants), that crucial twist never occurs, and you can end up with something called a volvulus, which sounds like a kind of Swedish superhero but is actually a dangerous condition in which the intestines get kinked, like a garden hose, and the path of digestion is cut off, restricting blood flow. You must have your belly split open so that everything can be put back in the proper order, or else you will die. If you're among the lucky souls born with properly ordered bowels, you should thank those bowels the next time they process a two-pound burrito on your behalf.

They found out that the baby had the condition when he began vomiting thick green fluid after his first feedings. The bile that he secreted to digest his formula was getting clogged in his intestines and was gurgling back up into his stomach, causing him to vomit over and over again. They placed a tube down into his stomach to suck up all the excess fluid and hoped the issue would resolve itself. Nights before the surgery, I stood by his isolette—an enclosed plastic incubator—in the NICU and stared at the output of that tube, praying that it would turn yellow or clear, hoping to God that he'd be spared the knife and that I'd never see that horrible green shit come out of him again. But I did see it again. I would come to the NICU during the day and ask the nurses if he barfed, my fingers crossed tight enough to break. And they often said yes, he had an "emesis." The first time I heard the word, I asked them if "emesis" meant barf, and when they said that it did, I wished they had just said that he had barfed instead.

The vomiting wouldn't stop. His insides weren't going to just naturally fall back into place. He had to be opened. No one makes it through life unscathed, but you usually get a grace period at the start. My son would not be so lucky. At the time, he weighed five pounds—large for a preemie, but still just five itty-bitty pounds. No heavier than a dictionary. I wondered how the surgeons' blades and instruments would fit inside him. *Such a large surgery for such a tiny body*, I thought.

The surgeon was talking us through the procedure as we all stood by the door to the OR. He had only a few moments to speak with us before our son had to go under. To wait any longer risked killing him.

"What's the survival rate for this surgery?" I asked the surgeon.

"If I don't find any salvageable bowel, the survival rate is zero." Doctors never explicitly say your loved one will die. They say things like "the survival rate is zero." It's up to you to jump to the proper conclusion. "But if the bowel is healthy," he said, "the survival rate is one hundred percent." He suspected my son's bowels were still viable, but he didn't rule out the possibility that there would be "dusky bowels," parts of the intestine that had lost blood flow permanently and were now dead and would have to be removed. Forever. I had never heard the term "dusky bowels" before. It sounded like a good name for a fantasy football team.

The doctor needed our consent before going ahead with the surgery. We didn't hesitate for an instant. In fact, we felt as if we had wasted enough of his time already. It's amazing how quickly you'll agree to a procedure like this once you hear talk of survival rates. You take a leap of faith. You trust that a total stranger will know how to properly disembowel your child because you do not. He was a nice-looking doctor. He seemed to know what he was talking about. *Fuck it.* I signed the forms.

The doctor rushed back into the operating room to prepare, and a very nice NICU nurse named Kathy led my wife and me to our son, to see him one final time before he went to have his guts torn out. They had knocked him out with an anesthetic, so he was sleeping peacefully by the time we got there. He was in an isolette and had wires running from his mouth, chest, stomach, and foot. He looked like an IED. He was surrounded by a phalanx of adults who were all determined to prevent his death because the death of a child is the saddest thing in the world. He wasn't old enough or awake enough to know that he didn't want to die. We did all that worrying for him. Kathy opened the top of the isolette so we could kiss him on the head—possibly for the last time, possibly just another kiss in an entire lifetime of them.

His head was coated with a shocking mass of black hair. When a baby is born premature, it still has plenty of the mother's hormones racing through its system. This can cause it to have enlarged genitals, lactating breasts (!!!), or a healthy head of hair. That hair eventually falls out and is replaced with new hair. But for now, our son still had hair long enough to get a side gig as a bassist. I bent down and let my nose glide along the soft fur, alternating between taking in his scent and kissing him on the head. I wanted to retain as much of the sensation as I could.

Kathy led my wife and me back out to the general surgical waiting room. They had updates on the status of all operations listed on a big monitor at the far end of the room. We could check on our son's intestines like we were trying to catch a connecting flight to Milwaukee. The second I saw my son's doctor and room number up on the board, I got a morbid thrill. *THERE'S MY BOY UP ON THE TEEVEE!* Then reality set back in and I could feel my heart withering. There were dozens of other people sitting in the room, and I felt exposed, naked, without any armor to protect myself. I just wanted to find somewhere for my wife and me to cry ourselves sick. Kathy saw us visibly breaking down in front of everyone and stole us into a private waiting room. I sat down next to my wife and stared off into space because the rest of the world seemed empty to me at the moment. Desolate. We took turns telling each other it was going to be okay because it helps in times of grief when someone you love tells you everything is going to be all right, even when you suspect that it's a lie.

All I could think about was my son dying. I tried my best to avoid it but I couldn't. I wondered what would happen if his intestines were deemed unsalvageable. *Do they euthanize your child? Do they just leave him until he starves to death because he can't fully digest anything? They can't do that. The world couldn't possibly be that cruel, could it?* I envisioned being escorted into the morgue and holding a swaddled, nine-day-old corpse in my hands, and how that would make me feel. He wasn't dead yet, but I had a clear idea of how badly it would hurt. My heart was firmly clenched to absorb the blow. I thought about whether we'd have a funeral for him. I didn't think we would because that would just be too awful to put our friends and family through. You can't herd people into a room and force them to stare at a tiny coffin for an hour.

I wondered if he could donate his organs as a premature infant. I wondered if we would bury him or cremate him, and where we might scatter his ashes. Maybe the Atlantic Ocean. He might like that. Maybe we would get a dog if he passed away, a little dog named Otis or Kirby that would bark and yip and shit all over the place and help us forget about this. That might help. Maybe nothing would help.

Maybe our marriage wouldn't survive if he died. We'd been married nine years, together for twelve. I remember the night we met, in some shitty Manhattan bar that no longer exists. I staggered out of the john and there she was, drunk and smiling, as if she had been planted there by some magnificent benefactor. It took five minutes for me to get her full name right because it was an obscure Armenian name and I was too shitfaced to pronounce obscure Armenian names. God, I loved her. Only an act of extraordinary circumstances could possibly end us: a war, a natural disaster, an unspeakable crime, etc. And as we waited, I thought that perhaps *these* were those extraordinary circumstances. Maybe we would look at each other after this and see nothing more than a reminder of what was lost. Maybe we would drift apart and I would become a filthy hobo, working odd jobs and dabbling in surfing and heroin.

I couldn't stop crying. My wife stood in front of me and I wrapped my arms around her waist and buried my head in her stomach. I told her all my fears in hopes that it would make us both feel better. I wanted to find a way *through* the grief, to emerge on the other side in a state of grace, knowing I was strong enough to live on regardless of what happened. But I still wasn't certain.

And then my wife farted—a remarkably well-timed fart that made me switch from tears to laughter right away. God bless that fart. I needed that fart. I asked her to do it again and she declined.

She went out for water, and a different nurse, who turned out to be a real shithead (every hospital has its share of dud nurses), told us that we were being kicked out of the private room. No more VIP treatment for us. When my wife came back in, we both took turns calling the shithead nurse a shithead behind her back, and then we headed out to the main waiting room. The receptionist said there was a phone call for us from the OR with an update. The doctor had promised us a mid-surgery update to let us know if the bowel was viable or not—if our son was going to live or die. This was that phone call. The receptionist held out the receiver for me.

I have a chronic case of Walter Mitty syndrome. I'm the type of person that spends an unreasonable amount of time during each day imagining himself plunged into extreme circumstances. Any time I walk outside with my children, I look up to the sky to see if a giant alien ship has stationed itself above my house. Any time I go to Target, I take note of which items I could use as weapons should a zombie apocalypse strike and then the entire store becomes a stronghold for the last of the uninfected. Any time I get on an airplane, I think about crashing in the ocean and being lost at sea for years, teaching myself to fish using only the stitching of my wallet. I am *constantly* foiling imaginary bank robbers and sexual predators. I waste hours every day envisioning a life far more dramatic, far more macho, than the sedate circumstances in which I usually exist.

That's part of the reason why I wanted to start a family. When you start a family, you're signing up for drama. You're signing up for worry. You're signing up for life-and-death. You're signing up for a life that means something more, even if it isn't as fun a life as when you were single and drinking shots of Fire Water in the Giants Stadium parking lot. Kids make your life significant. They give your life a spine. On some twisted level, I was signing up for a moment such as this: to be there waiting and weeping as I clutched my fists and begged for my son to be all right. But now that it was here, now that it was so sickeningly real, I knew I wanted no part of such cinematic moments. I just wanted life to become normal again. Uneventful. Boring. I wanted to go back to the intensely aggravating march of daily existence. I wanted my son to live so that he could grow up to annoy the shit out of me. People tell you that you should never take life for granted but that's wrong, because taking life for granted is an encouraging sign that your life is going well. I wanted *that*.

I took the receiver from the receptionist and braced myself.

SEVEN
YEARS
EARLIER

MERRIWEATHER POST PAVILION

My wife was pregnant for the first time, and I made extra sure to spend those nine months of gestation celebrating what I presumed would be the end of my freedom. When you're married without children, you're essentially still a single person. You can live cheaply. You can do drugs. You're mobile, with no goddamn kids anchoring you to one location. You can even get divorced with a minimum of fuss. If you're married and you don't have kids, you can drive to the beach on a whim. No living parent does that kind of thing. That's suicide. That shit requires ten months of intense planning.

So I took full advantage of the time I had left. My wife couldn't drink. She couldn't have caffeine. She wasn't allowed to have cold cuts because the bacteria on the deli slicer blade can get into the fetus and infect it with nine different strains of botulinum. She couldn't do much of anything. On the other hand, I could do as I pleased, and I did. I drank. I smoked all the weed I had left so that there wouldn't be any weed leftover in the house when the baby arrived because that was me being ethical. If this angered my wife, she was too busy retching into a mop bucket to show it.

Also, I bought concert tickets. Shit yeah, I bought concert tickets.

There was gonna be a big Oasis concert at Merriweather Post Pavilion, an outdoor venue located near Baltimore, forty minutes north of our house. Jet and Kasabian were the opening acts. This was back when listening to Jet was something people did. I bought two tickets because I assumed that once the baby arrived, I would be locked away from the world for two decades (NOTE: Not all the way true). I wanted to get drunk and go listen to Oasis because IS OASIS NOT THE GREATEST BAND IN THE WHOLE OF BRITAIN?

"I got these concert tickets," I told my wife.

"Oh, really?"

"Yep. Two tickets."

"Do you want to bring a friend?" she asked. I did.

"Well, I mean, I'd like to bring YOU. But if you think, *Whoa hey, this rock's too a-rockin' for me*, I totally understand."

This is a common and blatantly obvious trick men pull to kick their wives out of certain activities. *I'm gonna go to this thing, but totally feel free to not come. I leave that option to you because I am sweet and kind.*

"I'll go," she said.

"Okay. You sure?"

"Sure. Sounds fun."

"Double sure?"

"Yeah. Why? Do you wanna go with someone else?"

"What? No. That's crazy. Who better to share an evening of music with than my one true love?"

"Oh, please. Invite a friend."

So I did. Turned out none of my friends could go. But my wife still could, so off we went.

The seating at Merriweather Post Pavilion was broken in two. There were actual seats at the front, which were protected from the rain and which I could not afford. Behind those seats was a wide swath of grass where general admission folks could lay down a blanket, crack open an Igloo cooler filled with gin-and-tonics, and dance around like dirty hippies. We got to the lawn and virtually every available blade of grass was already covered. What's more, the two of us represented the smallest party going. Around me, there were groups of ten, twenty, even thirty people, already shitfaced and overly enjoying themselves as if they had been ripped right out of a Bacardi Silver commercial. I didn't know it was even possible to *have* that many friends, let alone so many friends orbiting you all at once. My wife and I found a tiny space to wedge ourselves into and we quickly realized that, even when you're a couple, you can feel a terrible collective loneliness. It's a kind of shared loneliness that grows even more pronounced once you've isolated yourselves with live children.

I'd like to take a moment here to let you know that first-time parents are fucking idiots. Part of the joy of being a veteran parent is watching new and prospective parents monkeyfart their way through the process for the first time. They're stupid. Understandably stupid, but stupid all the same. We were no different back then. We bought all the wrong shit for the nursery (an electronic paisley swing? SOUNDS ESSENTIAL). We felt compelled to take every hospital class even though hospital classes are useless and often feature disgusting video displays of colostrum leaking out of a decidedly nonphotogenic breast.

And we were far more overprotective of the fetus than we needed to be. My wife knew so many people who had experienced miscarriages—real, true, awful tragedies—that she was terrified of having one herself. I acquired that terror in turn. Hit a speed bump too fast? MISCARRIAGE. Divulge potential names to your mother too soon? MISCARRIAGE. Get in an airplane? YOU BETTER BELIEVE THAT'S A MISCARRIAGE. So when we arrived at this concert, we both were still on High Miscarriage Alert. But we managed to calm ourselves down and get excited about the show. I was into my fourth tall boy and very pleased that I had a designated driver for the evening.

Then Jet took the stage and set their amplifiers real, real loud. This was fine by me because ear pain lets me know the music is working. I started nodding my head like a good white person and then I looked over at my wife. She was traumatized.

"Oh my God! This is loud!" she said. I think she said it. All I saw were the lips moving.

"I KNOW! SO GREAT!"

"No! It's too loud!" She looked down at her belly, terrified that the guitars would somehow rawk the fetus right out of her. I rolled my eyes.

"Oh, come on. Really?"

She gave me the stink-eye. I immediately regretted the eye roll.

"What I meant to say is, you're totally right!" I said. We left the blanket and fled to the concession area, where the music couldn't get to us. "What do you wanna do?" I asked.

"I'm just . . . I'm a little scared."

"Well, do you wanna, like, leave? You don't wanna leave, do you?"

"Maybe I could call my doctor," she said.

"That's a great idea. You should call her. That would set your mind at ease and then we could enjoy the concert . . . TOGETHER."

"She might get pissed at me for calling."

"Screw that," I said. Doctors go to great lengths to guilt-trip every patient into not calling them outside of office hours. They have the whole trap set. They have that voicemail message that tells you to call 911 first. Then it says, "Well, if you *really* have to talk to the doctor, leave a message on our answering service." They give you every opportunity to feel like shit for bothering the poor doctor during dinner. It's a process designed to weed out the faint of heart. I refused to be cowed. "Don't feel bad about calling her," I said. "You pay those people hundreds of dollars every visit. Call the shit out of them."

"Okay," she said. "Then *you* call her."

"What? Me? Are you nuts? You're the patient. What would I say? I think you're the best person to handle this sort of thing. I believe in you." I was terrible at confronting people. Whenever I had an item to return to the store, I always asked my wife to do it because I was afraid the cashier would have me arrested for not having a proper receipt.

Now it was her turn to roll her eyes. She went to call the doctor's messaging service while I bought a beer, chugged the beer, and then bought another beer. I had planned on chugging *that* beer and then ordering another, but my wife came back, so I reverted to sipping.

"Is that a new beer?" she asked.

"No."

"It is, isn't it?"

"It is. Did you get the service?"

"Yeah, but now we have to wait here until she calls back."

"Maybe I should head back to our spot," I said. "You know, so no one takes it."

"You can wait five goddamn seconds, Drew. It's not even the main act."

At that moment, a particularly loud power chord rained down on us. My wife gripped her belly as if there were a bombing raid going on. Such was the power of Jet's second-hand riffs. I could see real fear in her eyes.

"I gotta get out of here," she said.

"You're overreacting."

"I don't feel safe."

"You could hang in the car while I stay here. The car's nice."

"Seriously?"

"Was that a poor suggestion?"

"YES!"

Another power chord. I caressed my wife's belly, shielding her from the musical onslaught, as if my back fat would somehow repel the sound waves. Now she was sick with worry. Her cell phone finally rang. I watched as she took the call.

"Hello? . . . Oh, hi, Doctor! So sorry to bother you at this hour! . . . Yes, yes, I think everything is okay! . . . Well, it's just that I'm at a concert, and the music is particularly loud. And I was wondering, you know, if extremely loud music could be detrimental to the fetus? Like, in any way?"

I saw her nod a few times and then hang up.

"What'd she say?" I asked.

"She said never to call her with something like this again."

"So you're okay?"

"Yes." She sounded disappointed. And frankly, I think I was too. I'd like to live in a world where rock and roll has the ability to cause spontaneous fetal ejections.

"So we're cool to go back to the concert?"

"I don't feel great about it."

"The doctor just said it was fine. You could fire a goddamn cannon next to your uterus if you wanted to."

"Well, I don't like it. I don't feel comfortable here. Is seeing some stupid band worth it, Drew?" She gave me a look that told me that I would have to choose between her and the music. And I didn't want to choose. I wanted both. I mustered up the very little courage I had and bravely stood up to an angry pregnant woman.

"Worth what? Worth you not magically aborting? YES. Totally worth it." I gestured to the crowd. "Come on," I said. "We're never gonna get to do this again. Let's have fun. I'm only being selfish so I can show you how much fun you can still have."

"Yeah, but you're also being straight-up selfish."

"That I am."

She looked back at me. "Gimme a sip of that beer." I couldn't give it to her fast enough. She took the tiniest of sips. Barely a vapor. A totally responsible sip of beer for a pregnant lady. "God, that's good."

"You see?" I said.

"Am I a crazy person for calling that doctor? I am, aren't I?"

"Not at all."

"Maybe a little."

"Maybe a little, yes."

"But she was kind of bitchy to me. And that's not right."

"Yeah! Who the hell is she to criticize you like that?"

"Jesus. I don't wanna be a crazy person."

I extended my hand. "Come on. This all goes away soon."

She took my hand and off we went merrily back to our spot. And we made it nearly halfway through Oasis's set before she got spooked again and dragged my ass out of there.

CHICKEN

The monitor was about to go off. It hadn't erupted just yet, but as I lay in bed I knew it was only a matter of time. You can tell when a baby monitor is about to blow up because the baby makes a series of pre-cry sounds that clue you in. Little hacks and scratches and cries—*ooooehhhh, durrrrr, ewwooohhhh*. Through the static of the monitor, it sounds like a mouse caught in a glue trap.

I didn't move a muscle. My strategy was twofold. For one thing, I thought to myself: *If I just stay still, then the baby will forget I exist and realize she has no one to cry to, and then she will stop crying* (NOTE: Babies do not fall for this). For another, I thought if I lay still long enough, my wife would get up and go feed the baby instead of me. I was awake, but I didn't want to be awake any longer. So I played dead. I tried to ignore the monitor and began thinking of purple unicorns and flying ninjas and any other random shit that would lead me to a dreamful slumber. Then I heard another *ooooooehhhhh* and my brain zeroed right back in on the monitor. *The child is waking. The child is hungry. Fuckity fuck fuck.* My wife was lying next to me in bed. She was perfectly still, an expert in not giving herself away.

Our first kid was now two months old. Before she was born, we prepared a bassinet for her. It was the same bassinet my mother-in-law had used for my wife when she was a baby and their family lived in Munich. My wife labored over successive weekends to restore it, sanding it down and repainting it clean white. The main basket had come loose from its wheeled base, so I lovingly repaired it, drilling new holes and driving in shiny new screws to make the bassinet secure, so that the girl could sleep peacefully next to our bed for as long as she liked. It was beautiful. I imagined night after night of her sleeping next to us, one little happy family tucked inside the little master bedroom of our little home.

The first night we put her in it, she screamed bloody murder for hours. Turned out she loathed it. We threw her in a crib in the nursery next door a few days later, and the bassinet became worthless. Babies don't give a shit how hard you worked on something. They're the harshest critics on earth.

We made a rule that we would take turns every night feeding her. Someone got the first feeding. Then, once the baby was back asleep, that person went to sleep and the other person handled the child the next time she woke up. That was a fair way of going about things. But on this particular night, we had forgotten to agree on who was gonna get the

first feeding. We both knew that who
ing was boned because the parent work.
to wake up around midnight, the time of
sleep takes root. And then, that same parent
get up again for a *third* shift, around 4:00 or 5:00

I didn't want the first shift. My wife didn't want to
shift. Someone was gonna lose.

A baby monitor is an inherently flawed product. You
don't really need one, but every family has one because every mom is terrified that she'll sleep through her baby's
cries and then the baby will starve to death in the middle of
the night and she'll wake up in the morning to find a stiff
baby corpse in the crib. This has never happened in recorded
history, ever. A baby is capable of crying loud enough to wake
a car accident victim hooked on fentanyl. All the monitor
does is *amplify* that crying, really driving those cries through
your eardrum so that they eat into your brain and make you
want to fucking die. Soon, the monitor enslaves you, sending
you running any time the baby so much as smacks her lips.

We bought a cheap First Years baby monitor at the Buy
Buy Baby. It was the only audio monitor they had left. The
rest of the shelf was stocked with video monitors, which
are expensive and pointless and scared the shit out of me because I imagined looking at the baby video monitor in the
middle of the night and seeing a ghost on the screen. The
forty-dollar audio one we bought had a series of lights on top
displayed in an arc. When the baby made a teeny tiny bit of
noise, the green lights on the left would light up. When the
baby cried a bit more, the yellow lights in the center would

ı in. And when the baby was crying like someone was
abbing her to death, the red lights on the right would engage. Right now, the lights were green. They would not remain that way for long.

Oooooehhhhh.

I remained motionless. My wife did likewise. Suddenly,
I realized that I had to scratch my face. I'm one of those
people who has to scratch himself in random places (including the scrotum) constantly, particularly right before bed. It's
like sleeping next to a meth head. If I didn't scratch my face,
I was gonna have a seizure. But I didn't want to give myself
away so I quickly clawed at my own eyes and then went back
to lying still, hoping my wife wouldn't notice. Then she
turned on her side. She had clearly taken my face scratch and
interpreted it as a sign that she had free rein to execute a
move of her own and then go back to pretending she was
asleep. But she wasn't asleep at all. She was faking it, which
outraged me despite the fact that I was also faking it.

Durrrrrr.

I could see the monitor firing up through my eyelids,
like flashes of lightning. Still, I said nothing. You could argue that lying in a bed listening to a baby monitor go nuts is
far more torturous than actually getting up and feeding a
child, but I wasn't having any of it.

Ewwooohhhh.

I scratched my face again and my wife turned again and
now everything was out in the open. One of us was gonna
have to back down, preferably before the real screaming
began.

Wahhhhhhhh!!!!

"Honey, can you get her?" my wife asked.

"No way," I said. "I had first shift last night."

"But you weren't with her all day like I was."

"What does that have to do with anything?"

"Please. I can't."

"What do you mean, you can't?"

WAHHHHHHHHHH!!!!

"I just can't," she said.

"Like, you're gonna literally die if you have to get up?"

"Will you please?"

"Oh, this is some bullshit."

I got up, turned off the monitor, and staggered out of the bedroom to the nursery. I cursed myself for trying to win a "Who's more tired?" argument with a woman. You're never more tired or more put-upon than she is. She did way more than you. And if you did more than her, well then she had to push that baby out of her vagina, which more than evens the score. It's a rigged game. I wished I could have carried the fetus to term myself just so I could have had that card to play for the rest of time. The pain would have been totally worth it.

The nursery had a changing table and a little caddy next to it that contained all of the bottles we would need for the night. There was also a small container that had three-ounce portions of formula powder in three separate chambers. We did this so that we wouldn't have to trudge downstairs in the middle of the night to make a bottle. It took us two months to figure out we should do this. Like I said, new parents are idiots.

I had to bring the bottle out to the bathroom to fill it with precisely three ounces of water. On the can of formula, there were harsh warnings about mixing it properly, so I was vigilant about getting the proportions right. I got a cheap thrill from being able to turn the tap off at the precise moment that three ounces of fluid had filled the bottle. It was like shutting off a gas pump right on a whole dollar amount. So, so exciting.

I turned on the water and waited for it to warm up. I could hear the baby's cries growing louder, even louder than when I first got out of bed. Babies have this incredible ability to throw you off your game with their cries. It's like being tongue-tied when you're talking to a beautiful woman. The harder they cry, the more of a fumbling mess you become.

"I'm coming! I'm coming!"

I hit the three ounces on the money, did a white boy fist pump, added the formula powder, capped the bottle, shook the thing like I was shooting craps at a casino, and then ran into the nursery. By now, the baby had turned deep red and was exhibiting homicidal tendencies. I grabbed her, plopped down into the glider with her, and jammed the nipple into her mouth. She began to slurp it down quickly. Too quickly. In the dead of night, I had to weigh my desire to go right back to sleep against my desire to not be coated in a gallon of curdled barf. I pulled the bottle away from my kid and she started going all berserker on me.

"Easy, girl. Easy."

I gave her the bottle back and let her get an ounce down before the ceremonial burping began. You have to burp a new baby after every ounce or so, or else they end up painting the walls with their insides. I tucked the bottle under my armpit to keep the formula warm (mmmm . . . armpit milk) and then put her on my shoulder. She instantly brought her knees to her chest, screaming with gas pain. I kissed her ever so gently on her face to calm her down, and for a brief moment I succeeded. She settled down and let out one of those beautiful little coos that only a newborn child can make. Then I nuzzled against her and stared into her big whale eyes and whispered to her that I loved her dearly, and that pissed her right off. I tried singing to her, in my most delicate singing voice, to calm her back down. I thought it could be a really beautiful moment between us.

"Hush, little baby, don't say a word . . ."

"WAHHHHHHHHHH!!!!"

"Daddy's gonna buy you a mockingbird. And if that mockingb—"

"WAHHHHHHHHHH!!!!"

"All right! All right! I'll stop."

She kept on crying and jerking her head around. Eventually, she gave me a full-on head butt and I recoiled in anger. I remember being furious with her, which is insane because how can you get mad at a baby? Oh, but you can. Late at night, when no one is watching, you can get obscenely angry at a baby. *You stupid fucking baby.* Sometimes you read about babies dying from shaken baby syndrome and you wonder, *Why would anyone want to shake a baby? How is this such a widespread problem?* And then your child head-butts you in the dead of night and suddenly there's a little voice in your head whispering to you, *Go ahead, shake that baby. Maybe shaking it gets all the tears out!* You just want the child to snap out of it and calm down, and you're willing to consider anything, even the stupidest idea. You feel like a monster merely for having the thought. It's almost as if the baby is testing you—putting you in the most pressure-packed situation possible to see if you make the right choices under duress.

I alternated between massaging the girl's belly and patting her back until she let forth a majestic belch that echoed through the nursery like a bell rung in a ballroom. It was a perfectly executed, adult-level burp. I had never been more proud. She was now asleep in my arms and I jammed the bottle back into her mouth so that she would unconsciously take the rest. I propped her head up with my left hand so that she would stay upright, and I could feel my arm begin to ache under the strain of the baby's giant head. It was like her skull was made of cast iron. I stared daggers at the bottle, watching the fluid drain down further and further, the fontanel on top of her head pulsing along with each sip. *Almost there. So, so close.* I was so excited to go back to sleep, I could hardly stand it. When a baby finishes a bottle, you can hear the nipple squeak like a dog's chew toy because all the formula is gone. It's the sweetest sound in the world because it means that you can finally get up and get on with your life. I was angling for that sound. I burped the girl again at the one-ounce mark and now it was only a matter of time. The formula kept going down, and then, just as I was about to hear that gorgeous squeak . . .

Thpppppppppppppppp . . .

A shit. A big ol' shit. It was almost as if she had been holding it in until just now on purpose. I was at the end. I could have been in bed within three minutes. Instead, this.

Before you have children, you look upon changing diapers as some kind of disgusting task, one you do with your hand to your nose. But actual parents don't care about that. The poop is beside the point. You get alarmingly used to wet feces showing up in random places. *Oh, it's on the stove. That's curious.* It's the disruption that changing a diaper causes that makes every parent hate it. I knew that changing the kid's diaper would fully awaken her and leave me stuck rocking her back to sleep for the next seventy minutes. I was screwed. I had to change the thing.

Or did I? After all, the baby was still sound asleep. Why disturb her? Wouldn't that be cruel? And hey, poop is warm. Everyone likes being warm! Maybe it would be okay to leave that puddle of shit in her pants. Maybe she liked it that way. And if she liked it that way, who was I to argue? You should do everything in your power to keep your child happy, right?

I put her back in the crib with a shit in her pants.

I sneaked back into the bedroom and turned the monitor back on. I sat on the bed ever so gently, so as not to disturb my lovely wife. My aim was to shut my eyes tight so that I could fall back asleep as quickly as possible. If I managed to fall back asleep, I would win. And the second I hit the pillow, the exact second my head touched linen . . .

Durrrrrr.

Was that her? Maybe that wasn't her. Maybe that was some other ambient sound, I thought to myself. This is always wishful thinking. If you suspect the baby is making noise, it's making noise.

Hack.

Maybe she's just settling back in, I thought to myself. She was quiet for a moment after that, and I lulled myself into believing my work was done. I was in the clear now.

Hack hack hack.

"Shit."

I got back up and trudged out of the bedroom. I made sure to sound extra huffy so that my wife would wake up and have sympathy and take over for me, but no. She was down like a gunshot victim. I was on my own. I grabbed the baby and tried to quickly change her diaper, only it took me ten minutes to align the snaps on her footies properly. Every time I thought I had it right, there was a stray unbuttoned snap right around her crotch. She began to fuss louder. There was a bottle of infant gas drops right by the changing table and I squirted an unknown amount into her mouth. I did this often. I don't think the gas drops had any medicinal value at all. They were probably just powdered sugar mixed with water. But at least it was something. She spit out the drops and kept on crying. I grabbed a swaddling blanket and wrapped her up extra tight, as if I were putting her in a straitjacket. *MWAHAHAHA. You'll never escape from the clutches of this fluffy giraffe blanket now*, I thought. She broke free in half a second.

There was a trace amount of formula left in the bottle. Now, formula allegedly goes bad after being out for an hour. At this point, I had no idea how long I'd been awake. Could have been forty minutes. Could have been nine days. But making new formula involved mixing, like, a whole new bottle.

I gave her the old formula.

She sucked it dry and began to close her eyes. *Yes, yes, attagirl.* Then, just as I heard that wonderful squeak of the empty bottle . . .

Thpppppppppppppppp. Another poop.

"Are you fucking kidding me?"

I put her back in the crib anyway to see if she would sleep, but the second I placed her on the mattress, she began to writhe and contort and make pained faces. I thought about propping her up on a Boppy—a curved breast-feeding pillow we had stashed in the closet. You aren't supposed to do this. You're supposed to leave a baby in a crib alone, with no other accoutrements around, because it can roll into things like pillows and suffocate. If I propped her up on a pillow, she might die. Then again, I was very, very tired.

I propped her up on a pillow.

She lay perfectly still there. So small. So beautiful. So silent. I loved her so very much, especially when she didn't make any noise. When you have a baby, you're always convinced that there's some kind of magic bullet that will get the baby to eat and sleep and behave properly. *OMG, all I had to do was put her on a pillow! Child: solved!*

I closed the door and the baby began screaming instantly. I went back in and tried putting a pacifier in her mouth, but she was crying and shaking her head back and forth and her mouth became a moving target. There was audible evidence of a mouth present, but goddamn if I could find it. I took a finger and scoured her face in the dim light for a set of lips, then managed to sneak the pacifier in. She spit it right back out. Babies aren't stupid. They know what you're trying to pull. They don't want you taking shortcuts.

I picked the girl up and changed her diaper again. She immediately threw up onto the changing pad, so now I had to engage in bodily fluid triage, trying to figure out if the shit should be wiped up first or the spit-up. I chose the shit, changing her diaper first and then giving her a new outfit. But she wouldn't stop going nuts. Maybe she needed food. Maybe she needed to make up for the milk she'd just spit up. I know I always like eating right after vomiting.

"Do you want more to eat? Is that what you want?"

WAHHHHHHHHHHH!

I got her more to eat.

I went to the bathroom and filled up a new bottle. At this point, I was failing in my efforts to remain half-asleep. I did my best to remain partially comatose so that, whenever this ordeal was over, I would fall right back asleep. But that hope was dashed now. I was legitimately awake. I took the baby down to the TV room and fed it while watching a Food Network show on mute, holding the bottle awkwardly, like when a child feeds a baby goat at the petting zoo. She wasn't interested in the milk. I stood up and walked around with her to calm her down, but she kept right on crying. I grabbed another pacifier and wiggled it around in her mouth, as if to anchor it in the back of her throat. She spit it out, so I put it back in again and held her close to my chest so that spitting out the pacifier was physically impossible. My spine was quietly falling apart. I had already had two operations on my back, the second one coming two weeks before the baby was born. My then-pregnant wife saw me lying on the hospital gurney before my operation and was like, "It's supposed to be ME on that thing, you bastard." My back was not yet equipped to handle the yeoman's work of carrying a baby around constantly, but the baby clearly didn't give a shit about my troubles. "Please fall asleep," I begged her. "Please, please, please. I'll do anything. I promise I'll never try to sing to you again."

But she just went on crying. I mouthed a quiet *fuck it*, took her back into the nursery, and put her in the crib, still crying. You aren't supposed to let a baby cry out the night until they're much older, around three to six months. Leaving a crying two-month-old is thoughtless, selfish, and cruel. But again, I was very tired.

I left.

I went back to the bedroom and didn't bother to turn the monitor back on. My thinking was: *If a baby is crying and no one can hear it, is it* really *upset?* I thought not. My wife, who was supposed to be sleeping, was quick to let me know she didn't share my viewpoint. I don't know how she managed to wake up after *not* hearing something, but there you have it.

"You have to turn the monitor back on."

"No way. I'm not turning that thing back on."

"Fine. Then I'll get the baby."

She got up and started walking out.

"Wait!" I said. "Does this count as your shift? Because this totally shouldn't count as your shift."

"Go to bed, Drew."

And I did. I slid into bed and it felt as if the bed were embracing me, as if I were nestled in the palm of some greater supernatural being. So soft and warm, I wanted to die inside of it. Nothing could pull me away. My wife was with the child now, but they were far away, in some other universe where things are loud and turbulent and nothing like the land of purple unicorns that I was entering. I became a nucleus: a tiny, impossibly dense thing tucked down into a void so expansive that the nearest particle seemed to be a million billion miles away.

Three hours later, the monitor went off at previously unknown decibel levels.

WAHHHHHHHHHHHHH!!!

I lay perfectly still. My wife lay perfectly still.

Hack hack hack WAHHHHHHHHHHHHHH!!!

"It's your turn," my wife said.

"What? No way. It was my turn last time."

"But I relieved you, so now it's your turn again."

"Are you joking? You were the closer. I did all the hard work. That doesn't count as a full shift."

"I was the one who was up last."

"This is an outrage!"

"Please."

"No."

"Please."

"No."

WAHHHHHHHHHHHH!!!

No one moved. The bed was far too comfortable.

GYMBOREE

My wife signed our daughter up for a gym class because she had to get out of the house with her. That's the biggest challenge of owning a one-year-old: You're constantly looking for ways to fill up the day. I was working in an office at the time, so this was of no concern to me. I got to go to work and talk to other people and dick around on the Internet and take a whiz whenever it suited me. I wasn't the one stuck with a one-year-old all day. The child was close to being ambulatory now. It could be taken out. It had to be taken out.

The brochure said that the classes helped toddlers with coordination, but that was mostly a ruse. They just provided a room full of padded, germ-ridden crap that toddlers could run around and fall down in. The main reason parents sign up for this kind of class is because it gives them a chance to relinquish primary control of the child to a peppy twenty-five-year-old gym teacher for forty minutes while they talk to other mothers about what a pain in the ass everything is. My wife loved the Gymboree class. If we had had the resources, she would have signed the girl up for it every day of the week. Not only did it give my wife time to rest, it also sucked all the energy out of the child so that she was perfectly set up to nap later in the day. Children have sixty times more energy than functional adults, and all that energy needs to go somewhere. Best that it goes into shaking a dirty parachute with a group of strangers.

I got home from work the day of the first class and my wife was overjoyed.

"Drew, it's so great. I don't have to do much. I even got to read a magazine for two minutes."

"That's great."

"You should take her."

"I'm not gonna be the only dad there, am I?"

"What? No. Of course not."

"Were there any other dads there when you went?"

"No, but that was a weekday class. I'm sure the weekend classes are different."

"All right," I said, piling up metaphorical brownie points in my head. "I'll take her. You stay here and relax. Take some sorely needed time for yourself."

"Actually, I have to do the laundry."

"NO, NO, NO," I said. I wanted this gesture to count. If she spent all that time doing housework, then I wouldn't have any excuse to demand free time of my own later on. For every hour a mother gets to herself, a father will demand five times that amount for drinking with friends and acting like an immature dipshit. "Don't do the laundry," I said. "You work real hard. Watch TV. Take a spa day."

"I have to do her laundry or else she'll have no clothes to wear and she'll throw up on her own naked body."

"Then I'll do the laundry."

"You suck at laundry," she said.

"Is it that I suck at laundry or that YOU suck at teaching me laundry?"

"Just take her to the goddamn class."

And so I did.

From the parking lot, I saw nothing but a mass of yoga pants and strollers heading for the gym. There's something inherently terrifying about knowing you're going to be the only dad at one of these things. I would be parenting in front of a live studio audience consisting of nothing but women. I mean, I was a real father. I handled feedings and played peekaboo and talked baby talk. I did all that, but the crude stereotype of the modern American father is that of a clueless dumbfuck who couldn't mix a bottle of formula even if the instructions were tattooed on his penis. I imagined the mothers judging me in the class, watching me carefully for any glaring fuckups. *Oh, look at the poor dad. Trying to act like a competent parent. How pathetic.*

Well, I wasn't gonna take that shit lying down. I wasn't gonna be a slave to the American Mother Hypocrisy Complex—this group of women who demand that men do their fair share but still want to be considered the superior caregivers. I was gonna ROCK THAT CLASS. I was gonna get down on that dirty mat and sing and hold hands and play all kinds of crazy baby games with the girl. And then all the women in that class would be simultaneously ashamed and turned on.

I got the girl out of the car, took her in my arms because she wasn't fully walking yet, and marched straight to the elevator. The door was still open, and a new mom and her mother were standing inside with a little boy. I confidently strode to the elevator with the girl in the crook of my arm. And right as I crossed the threshold, the door began to close and I bashed the girl's skull right into the side of it. You could hear the smack from across town. Sounded like someone dropped a crate of oranges out of a window.

"OH FUCK," I yelled.

The girl began to scream as the doors shut. Not a standard baby scream. The kind of scream that turns heads from a mile away.

"Oh my goodness!" said the mother's mother.

There was a blue horn growing on the girl's forehead.

"Can I help you?" the mother asked me.

"NO! No, everything's fine! She's just fine!"

"She sounds like she's hurt," the grandma said.

"Oh, you know . . . ," I said. I didn't even know what I was saying. I bounced the girl up and down and stared at the floor, hoping that staring at the floor would render me invisible. It did not. The two women could totally still see me. The elevator ride never seemed to end. I wanted the cables to snap so we would plummet down to the ground and this would all be over.

We finally got to the top floor and I walked into the class. The girl was still erupting. A dozen mothers turned and stared at me. There I was, the shithead father. I had already failed. I had justified all the stereotypes. I could hear them thinking about how incompetent I was. *Awww, that poor girl. Such a shame she has a negligent ass for an old man.* I felt the urge to flee, to run to a nearby bar and eat nachos for exactly forty minutes before taking the girl home and telling my wife that our day at Gymboree had gone just super.

But I couldn't. I wasn't gonna give up and turn tail in front of the coven, confirming their worst fears. I was representing American fathers here. I was their ambassador. I would be goddamned if I was gonna fail. But mostly, I hoped the class would get my daughter to stop crying.

The Gymboree class was housed in a nondescript room inside a shopping plaza, with the standard fluorescent lights and gypsum ceiling tiles. You could have moved everything out and converted the gym into an empty space for lease in less than thirty minutes. We found ourselves greeted by kiddie tunes blasting from a twenty-dollar boom box resting on the floor mat. A receptionist had me sign in and give my phone number. Parents have to do this in case they decide to go get a taco and the gym suddenly bursts into flames. I signed the form while the girl was crying. She was the only fussy child in the room, and I desperately wished that another child would throw a shitfit so I didn't look like the only person who didn't have control of his offspring.

A young instructor named Cassie, wearing the official Gymboree T-shirt, escorted us out onto the floor and instructed us to sit in a circle with the rest of the class. I kissed my daughter's new unicorn horn and made little hisses and buzzes in her ear—the kind that are supposed to help soothe fussy babies. But she was a toddler now. She wasn't buying any of that shit anymore. She wailed on and I began to fear that she would keep bawling and bawling until her fucking head exploded. I offered her a pretzel rod from a ziplock bag of now-warm snacks that had been sitting in my jacket pocket for three days. She smacked the pretzel out of my hand and kept on crying. I whisked her over to a corner, where she wouldn't be overwhelmed by all the other people around.

"Do you hear the music?" I asked her. "Isn't this fun?" I kept waiting for the part where I could get up and go read a magazine.

She let up crying for a second and I sensed an opening.

"See?" I said. "It's not so bad." There was a giant cylindrical pad over in the corner of the room that looked like a padded log. *Everyone loves logs!* I pointed at it. "Look at the log! I bet you get to play with it."

"Eeee!" she said happily.

"There's my girl! You're you again! Come on. Let's sit."

We sat back down and Cassie the instructor summoned us all to attention. Just the sound of a new voice was enough to get my daughter to ignore her lump and focus on something new. Teachers at all levels have a remarkable ability to get the attention of a roomful of children. I can't do that. If I try to gather up a group of drooling one-year-olds, they end up farther apart than when I started. We went around the room and introduced ourselves and our children. I had a name tag on. Name tags make any gathering six times more awkward and horrible.

"I'm Drew, and this is my daughter."

"Welcome, Drew!" said Cassie. "So nice to see a dad here today."

She jacked the boom box up to Oasis-concert volume and busted out all kinds of dirty used blocks and rattles for the kids to play with. In a matter of minutes, our cozy little circle of parents and toddlers broke apart as the kids rolled and crawled and spazzed out in different directions. I looked around at all the little padded ladders and trampolines, and I wanted a ray gun to shrink me down to half my size so that I could go play around on them. Then Cassie busted out the superlog and my daughter's transformation into a happy child was complete. Cassie lined the kids up on one side of the log and made them roll it across the room. Half of them stumbled and did soft faceplants on the floor, which I found highly amusing.

Then the child of the woman in the elevator started to cry and I felt a wave of triumph pass over me. I looked down at my daughter and she was now fully recovered from getting her skull dented. She had no memory of the incident, and she never would. We could start fresh. We could always find a way out of pain and unhappiness.

For the grand finale, Cassie dragged out the Gymboree-standard parachute, which had clearly not been washed in over a decade. All the little kids and parents gripped the diseased edges, lifting it up (with the parents doing the bulk of the work), then pulling it back down very quickly so that we could all hide under it, as if we were huddled inside a makeshift FEMA tent shelter. Then we got out from under the parachute and let the kids crawl out to the center so that the parents could shake it, the kids rolling around inside the chute like marbles in a dish. Cassie busted out an economy-size bottle of bubbles and blew them into the air while we all sang . . .

> There are bubbles in the air, in the air
> There are bubbles in the air, in the air
> There are bubbles way up high
> Way up high in the sky
> There are bubbles in the air, in the air

And my daughter floated out of class as if trapped inside by a bubble herself. There were other children who didn't make it through the whole class because they freaked out. Oh, but I had outlasted them all. I had struck a blow for confused fathers everywhere. I *won*.

But we took the stairs back to the car. No way I was fucking with that elevator again.

SLOW GUY

Our daughter was two years old now, so this was her first real Halloween. You can keep your children away from candy for the first two years of their lives. But eventually, once they're old enough to recognize what Halloween is and why it's there, the evil executives at Big Candy dig their hooks into them. All it takes is one little Reese's cup. After that, they're ruined forever. You may as well trade them in for new children.

I asked the girl what she wanted to be for Halloween.

"School bussy," she said.

"Okay," I said. "Are you sure? A school bus?"

"School bussy."

"That won't be easy. I'm not sure the CVS has, like, school bus costumes. You could be the bus *driver*."

"School bussy."

"A princess?"

"School bussy."

"I got it: Supergirl."

"School bussy."

Federal mediators couldn't have broken the stalemate. I went to my wife.

"Oh, I can make her a school bus outfit," she said.

"You can? How?"

"Haven't you ever made your own Halloween costume?"

"No. What am I—a Quaker?"

"It's more fun to make a costume. What do you wanna be?"

"I have to be something? I don't have to be anything. I'm a father now."

"Oh, come on. You have to be something. Something clever."

"Like what?"

"Well, we could put a really big penny on top of your head, and then you could be A Penny For Your Thoughts."

"Is that a costume or an art installation?"

"It's a suggestion. That's all."

I spent the next day exhausting every last ounce of creative energy trying to come up with a decent costume idea. The last time I had dressed up for Halloween was years earlier, when I was Popeye and my wife was Olive Oyl. I wore a red striped shirt and took a hollowed-out coffee can and wrote "SPINACH" on it. Then I drank beer out of the can and smoked weed out of the corncob pipe I bought from a nearby bodega. I could taste little coffee grounds in the beer. I ended up booting into the toilet at 2:00 A.M. that night. It was a really solid Halloween. Thus, I endeavored to come up with a similarly acceptable costume.

Meanwhile, my wife went to the art store and bought all the yellow poster board she could find. She cut out the sides and the grille and the windshield of the bus, and pasted black construction paper cutouts onto the sides for windows. Then she showed it to me.

"What do you think?" she asked.

"It's amazing," I said.

"No, it's not. The taillights need work." There's nothing that wives enjoy more than asking you your opinion and then immediately ignoring it.

She pasted on two red taillights, and I'll be damned if the thing didn't resemble a working school bus. If I had tried to do something similar, the child would have gone out into the street with an empty Asics box strapped to her head. This was the sort of thing only a mother could pull off. Once they've borne children, mothers can construct virtually any costume using scissors, felt, Elmer's glue, and a leftover pen spring. They're like the Special Forces of crafts.

The neighborhood we live in has no sidewalks, so weeks earlier my wife had purchased a big yellow plastic SLOW sign in the shape of a crossing guard that was thirty-two inches high, all in the name of slowing down passing motorists. She felt compelled to buy it after two teenagers in a van went tearing down the street while my kid was playing outside. I mouthed at the kids to slow down (I even made the classic "STOP" move with my hands, raising both palms like I was a palace guard halting an intruder). In return, one of the little fuckers leaned out of the window and extended a double bird, and then they both screamed, "FUCK YOU!" Then they hit the gas even harder, banked around the curve at the end of the street, and screamed, "FUCK YOU!" a second time. I turned crimson with Old Man Rage, vowing to throw rocks at the car if I ever saw it again. Not only was I pissed that they'd told me to go fuck myself, but I was also doubly angry that I had evolved into the kind of middle-aged dipshit who yells at kids to slow down. That should've been ME tearing down the street with a joint in one hand listening to "Rocket Queen." I wanted to buy a shotgun and sit out on my stoop every night until they came speeding by again. My wife bought the SLOW guy sign instead.

At a loss for a decent costume, I noticed the SLOW guy wore a red cap. Then I remembered I had a yellow T-shirt. So, the day of Halloween, I scrawled "SLOW" in black marker across the front of it, and then I bought a three-dollar plain red cap from the drugstore. When fully assembled, the "costume" didn't make me look like the SLOW guy. It made me look like *a* slow guy. The hat should have had a propeller on top. I became terribly concerned that wearing the costume made it look like I was making fun of special-needs children, especially when paired with a child walking around dressed as a shortened school bus.

But it was too late to change anything. Trick-or-treating time was getting closer and this was all I had. I was stuck with being the SLOW guy. No way was I going back to CVS to buy more crap. My wife threw on her costume (she was Lady Gaga, because you can put yourself in virtually any ugly outfit and declare your costume to be a Lady Gaga costume) and we were set to go. Then I realized that, while scrambling to accidentally dress myself as a retarded child, I had forgotten about the bags and bags of candy my wife had bought at the grocery store and then stashed out of my reach.

"Hey, what do we do about giving out candy?" I asked. "We're not gonna be here."

My wife grabbed a metal bowl from under the sink. "We can use this," she said.

"Do we need a sign?"

"Probably."

I raced to make a sign for trick-or-treaters, instructing them to take just two pieces of candy (my wife turned down my idea of adding "WE WILL BE WATCHING YOU" to the end of the message). Then I tore open the bags, dumped in the candy, and ate three peanut butter cups in the span of half a second.

"I see you!" said my wife.

"I'm a man, dammit! I'll eat candy if I want to."

"You have chocolate on your SLOW shirt."

"Shit."

Despite its flawless construction, there were issues with my daughter's school bus costume. My wife had cut a piece of ribbon and bored two holes on either side of the bus. Then she tied the ribbon through each hole so that we could hang the bus on my daughter's shoulders. When I put it on the girl, she turned and knocked the bus into the TV set. Its life flashed before my eyes. *Holy shit, no. Not the TV.*

"Let's just put this on you outside," I told her.

Once we got outside, it was clear that the girl had limited mobility with the box hanging on her. Every time she went down a concrete step, I became terrified that the box would trip her and she'd end up eating the curb. I had a clear picture of it in my head, watching her fall and seeing her teeth shatter and her lips tear open. Blood everywhere. Scars. Lifetime deformities. I couldn't stop seeing it, so I grabbed her hand. She immediately recoiled. My palms were very hot and clammy and she was able to escape them easily.

"No hand!" she screamed. She was under three feet tall and already a far more assertive human being than I was.

"You gotta take my hand. I don't want you tripping and falling and dying."

"NO!"

She ran ahead and I saw my wife go after her, finally convincing her to take her hand, since a mother's hands are dry and soft and pleasant.

There was a group of parents congregating down the street. The plan was for all of the kids to go trick-or-treating together so that all of the adults could hang out and, in theory, socialize. We met up with the group, and one of the neighborhood moms asked me about my costume.

"What's your costume?"

"Oh, this? I'm a SLOW guy."

"A slow guy?"

"Not, like, a retarded guy. I swear. You know how we put a sign outside our house because those asshole kids drive too fast?"

"Not sure I saw it."

"Well, it's like this little guy and he says 'SLOW' and he has a red cap. So that's me."

"Oh! Oh, that's very clever."

"Oh, thank you. And again, *not making fun of retarded people here.*"

With every subsequent conversation, I felt compelled to explain my costume immediately, as a preventive measure. I was already socially awkward around other parents, and this added a fun new wrinkle to my discomfort. The moms fell in together and began talking shop about bedtimes and their kids' eating habits. Moms are excellent at this sort of thing.

Dads, on the other hand, interact like a dozen horses tied together at the head. I shook hands and stammered out a couple of empty *how you doin'*s, but I wasn't giving it my full effort because I was still a relatively new father. And new fathers despise talking to other fathers. I withdrew. My daughter was bumbling around in her school bus outfit and I stayed by her because hanging with your kids is such an effective way to be antisocial.

Then I noticed another dad walk up with a giant wagon filled with cold beer and I saw salvation. I didn't know the dad well, but I had failed to bring out any beer of my own, which was an incredible oversight. I made getting beer a priority.

But then the trick-or-treating started. The sun began to fall and you could hear joyous squeals from kids ringing out from all around the neighborhood. Little flashlights strobed around up and down the street, and I heard the older kids plotting which house to hit next. I held a flashlight out in front of my daughter, but the bus was still causing her problems and she was dragging her candy bag along the ground. My wife was busy cavorting with her friends so I was left to hunch down and make sure every step the girl took wasn't her last. Meanwhile, the beer wagon set off in the opposite direction. I knelt down by the girl and tried to turn her around.

"Maybe we should go this way, dear."

"No."

"There's more candy that way."

"No."

She stopped at a nearby house that had fifty-three steps leading up to the front door. She may as well have declared her desire to scale Everest. The front stoop was tiny, almost as if it were designed so that a simple outward push of the screen door could wipe out hordes of trick-or-treaters.

"That's too many steps, sweetheart. The other houses have candy too."

"No."

"What if we take the bus off of you so you can climb those steps safely?"

"No." Gather together a hundred of the finest lawyers and you wouldn't have as formidable a negotiating entity as a two-year-old.

I took her hand and gingerly walked up the stairs, the

beer wagon getting farther away with every step. Midway through, my daughter slipped and I held her hand tight as she dangled in the air and righted herself, as if she were hanging from a cliff. The school bus outfit continually banged against the flagstone steps and eventually I stooped down to keep it raised as the girl ascended the staircase in full. The descent looked precarious.

We got to the top and I said a big "HI!" to our neighbor, a nice woman who held out a basket that had a handful of peanut butter cups scattered among all the Smarties and lollipops and Jolly Ranchers. The girl went straight for the shitty candy. I tried to steer her toward better options.

"You sure you don't want one of these peanut butter cups? Ooooh, Baby Ruth! I haven't had one of those in ages!"

"No."

"You sure? It's chocolate. MMMMM, CHOCOLATE."

"No."

She grabbed two generic lollipops and we carefully descended the steps. I was already tired and this was only the first house. Then one of the older girls in the neighborhood— who babysat the girl from time to time—walked up to me. She was surrounded by a group of friends. My daughter stared up at them in awe.

"Hi, Mr. Magary."

"Oh, hi."

She looked down at my daughter. "Do you want us to take her around?"

"Her costume's a little rough to handle."

"Oh, I can just take that off."

She bent down and lifted the bus away with no resistance from the girl. Before I could say anything more, she was leading the girl from house to house to pile up candy. I stood there with my flashlight and watched my daughter go off into the distance, the world filling up around her as the collective wail of all the kids in the neighborhood grew louder and louder the more they ate. I could hear the girl's laughter close by and I could feel the knots in my shoulders begin to slack. Then I got a tap on the shoulder and wheeled around to see my neighbor. He had the beer wagon.

"You want a beer, Drew?"

"Hell yeah. Thanks."

He handed me the bottle and looked over my costume.

"So what's the costume?"

"Oh, me? I'm a slow kid."

He laughed. "That's tasteful. Cheers."

We clinked bottles and melted into the group of other dads, and after a while I stopped worrying about whether I looked like a lame asshole with kids and instead luxuriated in being one. And when we got home, there was still plenty of candy in the dish waiting for me.

PRINCESSES AND PALESKINS

Miss Rhonda was the local ballet teacher—a short, cheerful woman who loved teaching little girls to dance more than anyone has ever loved doing anything. Once a week, my daughter went to Miss Rhonda for ballet class. I use the term "ballet" loosely here because you can't force two-year-olds into pointe shoes and demand they lose five pounds before *Swan Lake* dress rehearsals begin. You can only hand them costumes and let them run around a room to Disney music.

Prior to meeting Miss Rhonda, the girl didn't give a shit about princesses or princess culture. She was all about school buses and car washes. Take any two-year-old through a car wash and their skulls are blown. FLAPS! FOAM! ROLLING THINGS! It's the closest they'll ever get to being inside a working spaceship. The girl loved school buses even more, as demonstrated during the previous Halloween. One time, I bought her a big plastic school bus that was fourteen inches long. It cost five bucks. She named the bus Charlotte and slept with the thing every night. I tried to take it away from her once because she kept banging me in the shins with it, and when I did, she screamed like a mother having her child being led away by social services.

I took her inside a real school bus once and it was like a grown man being led onto the field at Yankee Stadium. She was awed. She treated the rows of cheap green vinyl seating like church pews, making a point of sitting in every single one. I made sure to show her the hump seat in the back, the one that rests over the rear wheel well.

"That's where the awesome kids sit and write out dirty Mad Libs," I told her. She nodded in reverence.

The day of her first ballet class, I ran into a mom who asked me if my kid liked princesses.

"No, she likes buses," I said, proud the girl had resisted the whole phenomenon. She wasn't a sucker like the rest of her peers. Her interests were *real*, not some byproduct of corporate brainwashing. "I don't think she really cares about princesses."

"Oh, she will," said the mom. She had a gleefully ominous air about her, as if she enjoyed the prospect of my future suffering.

Over in the corner of the church basement, Miss Rhonda kept a long rack of princess dresses, including favorites like Snow White, Cinderella, Sleeping Beauty, Jasmine, etc. All the little girls grabbed at the dresses like it was the first night of eliminations on *The Bachelor*, and my daughter followed suit. All she had to see were kids her age grabbing at the dresses to know she desired them.

From that day forward, the girl was all princesses, all the time. The Disney Princess people have made marketing inroads into every facet of American existence, and I was now forced to deal with all of them. They have princess stickers on *grapes*. They aren't special grapes, mind you; they're just grapes that happen to be marked up 200 percent. Suddenly, I saw princesses all over the place, hiding in plain sight. It's like when you buy a car and then suddenly see nothing but that particular car every time you go out driving. I wanted to refrain from buying her so much princess crap, but the girl just seemed so *excited* by it all. I didn't want to kill her buzz. No parent ever does. Suddenly, the whole culture had seduced not only my child but my wife and me as well. We bought all the princess movies. We bought all the princess games. We bought all the princess Barbie dolls. The girl forced me to personally dress the dolls on several occasions.

"I don't think this Princess Jasmine halter top will fit on Princess Aurora," I told the girl. "It's been tailored for a more . . . uh . . . buxom princess."

"Just do it!"

"Why are her hands so rigid? It's like she's dead. I can't get any of the fabric past her wrist."

There was no stopping the girl's descent into Princessmania. She loved all the princesses and she loved Miss Rhonda. Certain people have the touch when it comes to dealing with children, and Miss Rhonda had it. She knew which princess was each student's favorite at any given second. She offered to make princess dresses for my daughter. She even invited the girl to her end-of-summer party at her house. We ate that shit up. I felt like I had gotten in with the Mob. Miss Rhonda had tapped our child for greatness. We were IN. And while I despised the entire Princess Industrial Complex, I wasn't above flattery. When a teacher is paying extra attention to your child, you believe that it's because you raised such an exceptional kid, one that stands out head and shoulders above the rest of her booger-eating friends. *Let's see little Brandy Reynolds down the street get that kind of audience with Miss Rhonda!*

At the end of ballet season, all the parents were invited to come watch the students perform a recital. The theme of this recital was Pocahontas, one of the lesser Disney princesses but also one of the most attractive. Miss Rhonda dressed all the girls in Native American outfits and gave them headdresses made out of construction paper. She lined the girls up in an imaginary canoe and had them pantomime rowing down a river. As they heaved and hoed, Miss Rhonda suddenly stopped them.

"STOP!" she cried. "I hear the paleskins coming!"

I whispered to my wife, "Did she just say 'paleskins'?"

"I think she did," my wife whispered back.

"Is that racist? I mean, she's talking about white people, so that's okay, right?"

"Shhhh!"

The girls stopped pretending to row, and Miss Rhonda commanded, "Now say, 'What do you want, paleskins?'"

And all the girls shouted, "WHAT DO YOU WANT, PALESKINS?"

I turned to my wife. "Holy shit! Now they're all saying it!"

"Shhhh!"

Then Miss Rhonda assumed the role of the bad guy from the Virginia Company.

"I'm going to take all your land!" she shouted at them.

Well, the little Pocahontases weren't about to take being colonized lying down. They jumped up and chased Miss Rhonda all over the room while doing an Indian war chant, patting their mouths and making the stereotypical BABABABABA sound, which was just breathtakingly inappropriate. I gritted my teeth and prayed that no members of the Sioux Nation would stumble by the church basement window to see it. It was a revolution in miniature, and Miss Rhonda couldn't quash it with smallpox-infected blankets the way real settlers did.

Every month, my daughter latched on to a new princess to worship. She got so into Snow White that she would play the DVD and pantomime every scene in it. At night, she demanded that I tell her the story of Snow White getting lost in the dark and frightening forest, then she demanded I tell it again and again and again.

"And then Snow White got lost in the dark and frightening forest," I said. "And all the evil trees tried to eat her."

"No, no, no! They were nice trees!"

"They were?"

"Mmm-hmm."

"Because in the movie, the trees look pretty angry."

"No, when she wakes up, all her animal friends are there."

"Yes, and then all of the nice rabbits and deer showed up and Snow White was happy."

"Tell it again!"

"No."

Eventually, she asked me to download the soundtrack so that she could act out the movie on her own, without the pictures to guide her. All I had to do was say no, but again I didn't. I still liked the cheap sugar rush you get from buying your kids stupid crap. I downloaded the soundtrack, and over the next few weeks, the girl would have me play it front to back and watch as she acted out every scene. I got to be the Huntsman and pretend I was gonna stab the shit out of her multiple times, which I found inappropriately cathartic. My daughter also took special care with the scene where Snow White bites into the apple, dies, and rests in a glass coffin. The girl was all about resting in that glass coffin. One day, while we were playing in the basement, she explained the blocking needed to perform her Snow White routine.

"I'm going to die," she told me.

"Okay," I said.

"And then you're going to come and kiss me on the lips."

"Yeah, no, that isn't gonna happen."

"And then we can get married!"

"HOLY CHRIST, NO."

She grew serious for a moment. "Dad, am I gonna die?"

"Like, you personally? In real life?"

"Yeah."

"Not anytime soon."

"Are *you* gonna die?"

"Me? Not anytime soon."

"But when?"

"I don't know. Maybe when I'm eighty? Hopefully, we'll all be cyborgs by then."

"What's a cyborg?"

"The point is . . . you don't need to worry about dying anytime soon. That's the fun of being your age."

"Okay. Well, I'm going to die now."

"Okay."

She lay down on the couch as the chorale for Snow White's funeral pageant began playing. She closed her eyes and lay perfectly still, pursing her lips just a touch.

At a certain point, you learn to get over yourself as a parent. Diapers are gross, but you get over it. You go to bed at 9:00 P.M. every night because you're lame, but you get over it. And sometimes, your child will innocently want you to kiss her on the mouth, clearly not thinking of such an act the same way you do. You get over it.

The girl looked very pretty in her official Disney Snow White dress, lying pretend dead on the couch. The dress had poofy blue shoulders and cheap gold trim along the sleeves, with a sparkly red top and a silken sheath of yellow polyester for a skirt. The Christmas prior, my mom had bought her a pair of blue Snow White shoes, with blue heels that blinked with every step and a little heart-shaped picture of Snow White adorning the toes. She had her eyes closed and arms crossed over her chest now, and for a moment, I thought about what it would feel like if she really were dead, if that were really her corpse resting on the sofa, with a choir chanting, "To be happy forever." She was so beautiful and perfect lying there, the thought of it was unbearable. I wanted her to wake up, to live again.

I leaned in and gave her the tiniest of pecks. The girl's big fat brown eyes popped open and she smiled as if she really had been brought back from the grave. I led her out into the center of the room and spun her around as the finale played. In my head, I was fast-forwarding two and a half decades to her wedding day, seeing her resplendent in a white gown and leading her out onto the parquet floor of some random hotel ballroom, with her new husband—a strapping young lad who needed to kiss my ass for YEARS before finally winning my grudging approval—looking on. I could nearly touch the moment.

A few months later, I was about to take the girl to Miss Rhonda's class and she resisted.

"I don't wanna go," she said.

"You don't?" I asked. "Don't you like ballet?"

"No. It's boring."

"What about princesses?"

"Princesses are for little kids."

"Well, what do you like?"

"Alicia!" She pronounced it "*Ah-LEE-cee-ah*" in a fabulous Spanish accent.

"Who's Alicia?"

"FROM *GO, DIEGO, GO!*"

"Seriously? That show is awful."

"I wanna be Alicia for Halloween!"

So Alicia became the next phase. And then puppies. And then secret agents. And then some other thing. I've lost track at this point. We never went to Miss Rhonda's class again.

On a shelf in our basement, we still have all the remnants of her infatuations: Charlotte the bus, the dresses, a toy car wash my brother-in-law constructed for her. Each group of toys represents a phase in the girl's life that she'll never repeat, a person she'll never be again. Sometimes I miss those versions of her. Sometimes I have to fight the urge to listen to some dwarf song while I'm working because I want to get a whiff of the memory because the memory is the only real connection you have to that version of the child. Even a photo is hopelessly inadequate. I look at the photos now and find it hard to believe those phases ever existed. I need something tangible to unearth the feeling: a song, a dress, a magic wand, whatever. In my head, sometimes I can hear that choir at the end of *Snow White* still singing, and I can see the girl lying stone-dead on our couch. I miss seeing her like that. I miss having the chance to save her.

CAESARIAN

My wife and I agreed that we needed to have a second child because an only child is 90 percent more likely to have an imaginary friend who wants to murder you in your sleep. Besides, our daughter was getting older now and my wife wanted her to have a "friend" in the house, as much as a two-year-old can be friends with a baby that doesn't do anything but sleep and cry.

It took a year for us to conceive our second child. This is a common ordeal for the average middle-class American couple that puts off having children until their thirties. We knew so many other couples that had experienced fertility problems and miscarriages that it was more surprising when someone we knew had a child *without* being consigned to thirty-eight consecutive weeks of bed rest. Turns out God WANTS you to conceive when you're eighteen years old, apparently so that you can spend your twenties miserable and penniless and living in a camper.

Months passed and our frustration over failing to have a second child grew more acute. Every new period that arrived felt like a horrible defeat. *All that hot sex for nothing!* My wife asked me to go to a urologist and he told me that, when trying to have a baby, the male should only orgasm once every three days, in order to build up a hefty payload. You really wanna saturate the woman's reproductive area, like it's an Iowa floodplain. I tried holding out for three days at a time. It was not easy. By the second day of the abstinence cycle, I was ready to hump a mailbox.

Sometimes my wife's cycle would arrive a week late and we'd cross our fingers and hope that the pregnancy had taken root, getting our hopes up higher and higher the further we got away from the cycle date. Then the period would drop and the entire project would be reset. I felt like I was raking up a pile of leaves only to have the wind blow them all away. The process became torturous—the idea of a second baby finally arriving seemed so far away that I felt as if we would never get to it. We wanted every failed pregnancy test to be a mistake. *Hey, it came from Target. Just how reliable could it be?* Of course, the second we finally got a positive, we took the exact opposite stance. *Hey, it came from Target. It can't possibly be wrong!*

So it took a while to finally break into the bank vault and get my wife successfully pregnant again. By the time I got her to the hospital to be induced, we had essentially been waiting for the boy to arrive for twenty-one months. My wife didn't feel like waiting one second longer.

The nurse came into my wife's hospital room to check her cervix. It needed to be dilated to ten centimeters before she could start pushing the boy out. It was not at ten centimeters. It wasn't even close.

"We're gonna have to apply Cervidil," she told us. For those of you who are unfamiliar with the drug Cervidil, it is—according to its own website—a "vaginal insert for cervical ripening," which I think you'll agree makes a woman's cervix sound delicious. Cervidil must be applied directly to the cervix, which is akin to someone trying to jam a thumbtack into the back of your throat using a boxing glove. The nurse began the application.

"OH JESUS CHRIST!" my wife screamed.

"Almost there," the nurse noted.

Meanwhile, I stood there holding my wife's hand, being like, "It's okay, dear." And it so wasn't okay. I was of no help whatsoever. You never feel more useless than when your pregnant wife is screaming her brains out and you know that there's nothing you can do verbally or physically to make it better. The fact that you're standing there like an idiot—having the dumb luck to be born with a penis—only makes it worse.

The worst part was that the Cervidil was merely the beginning. The drug doesn't even induce labor. It only induces the inducement. You have to get it inserted overnight, wait twelve hours, have your cervix checked again, and

THEN you get the Pitocin, which is a drug meant to speed up the process. After the first application, we sat there bored out of our minds for half a day. I turned on the TV in the room.

"Oh, hey," I said to my wife. "It's *House*! We haven't seen this one!"

"I don't wanna watch a hospital show. I'm IN a hospital. Right now."

At that moment, one of the patients on the show started coughing up blood in her hospital room, and my wife nearly threw the remote at me.

She was strapped to two different machines, one that monitored contractions and another that monitored the baby's heart rate and blood pressure. The cheap Velcro straps began to dig into her skin. You can't lie flat on your back when you're in the late stages of pregnancy because it can restrict blood flow to the fetus. As a result, pregnant women have to contort themselves into a variety of positions, none of them optimal. My wife couldn't stand the discomfort one second longer. I stared at her belly and it seemed like it was its own separate entity, just this massive orb of flesh divorced from her body. I kept waiting for it to float away like a hot air balloon. Every time she wanted to take a leak, she had to rip the monitor equipment off, go to the bathroom, ask the nurse to resquirt her tummy with clear goo that looked like a porn film money shot, and have the monitor electrodes strapped back on. At one point, her eyes lolled back inside her head.

"I feel dizzy," she said.

"Are you okay?" I asked.

"I think I'm gonna pass out."

Her blood pressure began to drop precipitously and I ran out of the room to grab a nurse, only one was already walking over because nurses can monitor patients from the front desk, which is helpful for them because then they don't have to actually talk to patients. The nurse strolled in and looked at my wife.

"Hmm. That's weird," she said casually. "Her blood pressure is NOT supposed to be that low."

"Is she dying?"

"Huh. Why is this machine being so silly?"

I tried to strangle the nurse with my eyes. "IS SHE DYING?!"

The amazing thing about hospitals is how blasé the nurses and doctors can be about everything. An exploding heart is no more interesting to them than a bad sandwich. It's not like on TV, where doctors run EVERYWHERE, their asses tightly clenched and their faces grim with the determination to save lives, no matter the cost. In a real hospital, everyone just plods along. A patient is an item on a to-do list. If a patient is stable enough to be left unattended for twenty straight hours, then they can be left unattended for twenty straight hours. There's no constant sense of urgency.

Of course, doctors and nurses have to be this way. They can't be emotionally attached to every patient. They can't be screaming out for defibrillators every waking second. They'd end up doing their jobs poorly. I understood all that while we were in that room, and yet it was little comfort when my wife's blood pressure was dipping down to corpse levels and the nurse was acting like the fucking cable box was on the fritz.

She administered new meds through the IV and my wife shot back to life. Then the nurse left us to process what had just happened.

"Was I dying?" my wife asked me.

"The nurse never really made it clear."

"Because that felt . . . bad."

"You didn't look happy about it."

"Somebody needs to come take this goddamn baby out. I'm dying of thirst." When you're in labor, you can't eat. You can only suck on ice chips instead of drinking straight fluids. And ice chips are terrible—tiny little nuggets formed from what tastes like old dishwater. It's like chewing on a handful of frozen teeth. Refilling the ice chip cup every half hour was the only useful task I could perform for her.

A few hours later, the nurse came in and said the Cervidil had to be applied a second time. My wife nearly passed out hearing the news.

Sixteen hours after arriving at the hospital, she was finally ready to be induced. The anesthesiologist came by to administer the epidural and my wife greeted him as a liberator. Soon after, the ob-gyn came into our room for the delivery, followed close behind by my father-in-law, who had popped in for a visit.

The doctor looked over my wife. "Okay, so I think we're about ready to—"

"Excuse me, Doctor," said my father-in-law. "Are you Dr. Kleinbaum of the Rockville Kleinbaums?"

"Oh, yes."

"I think that your daughter is our neighbor at the beach!" My father-in-law is a wonderful man who hates waking up before 1:00 P.M. and loves having extended conversations with absolute strangers.

"Really?" asked the doctor.

"Yes! I think they live in the townhome right next door."

"Is that right?"

"How is she? We don't get down there much because we usually have to rent out the house during the summer. You know, they're making all kinds of noise about building on the lot next door—"

"HEY!" my wife shouted, pointing at her belly. "Pregnant woman here!"

My father-in-law took umbrage. "We're just having a nice conversation, *Schatz*."

"Will you get out of here already?"

"All right, all right."

He looked at me and laughed. "Good luck, Drew." Then he sauntered out of the room, as casual as if he had just gone shopping for groceries.

Finally, after hours of waiting for my wife to ripen, she was ready to push. The nurse took one of her legs and I hoisted the other. We pulled her legs back like she was a turkey waiting to be trussed as a second nurse sat sentry over the precious dilated cervix. She began pushing sometime around midnight. After a few hours of trying to pop the baby out, the thing had barely moved an inch. My wife looked exhausted. Defeated. She was looking for the doctor to finally walk back into the room (they don't have to be there for all of the pushing; doctors are just closers) so that she could end the charade of trying to have the child naturally. At this point, she wanted sleep and a cold ginger ale more than she wanted a second child. The doctor came back in, examined the crown of the baby's head, and offered my wife two options.

"Okay, so this baby isn't coming out," he told her. "And I see his heart rate dropping. So we can keep at this pushing for a bit, or we can—"

That was all the opening she needed. "CAESARIAN!"

"Are you sure?"

"Please. Just get this thing out."

They handed me a set of surgical scrubs, which I put on with glee because I love pretending to be a doctor. Then the nurse told me I had to gather up all of our stuff because we weren't coming back to the room. I looked around. There was a lot of shit. I didn't want to move. I hate moving. This was our home now.

"Can't I just leave it here for a second?" I asked.

"I'm afraid not," the nurse said.

"Well, where do I put it? Is there, like, a bus station locker somewhere?"

"They'll have a place for you to put your things in the recovery room."

I threw all of our belongings into six different hospital-issued garbage bags and then huffed alongside my wife like a homeless person as they rolled her gurney roughly ten feet to the OR. I was expecting a much longer walk, a walk long enough for me to make some kind of rousing speech about the beauty of this moment to a woman who was half-conscious. Instead, the OR was right there, which makes perfect sense from a medical standpoint, though not from a dramatic one. The recovery room nurse told me to place my bags on a nearby chair, and I begged her reassurance that no one would come and steal my wallet while my wife was being slashed open.

They put a shower cap on my wife's head and drew a curtain across the top of her stomach. The nurse told me not to go past the curtain, and I obeyed the hell out of her. A team of doctors gathered at her feet and the sounds began. I could hear gooshing and gurgling and all kinds of horrible noises. Not being able to look beyond the curtain only made things worse because it allowed my imagination to roam free, with scythes and ice cream scoops digging into my wife's body.

"Do you have the baby?" I asked the doctor.

"Not yet. Sometimes, once the incision is opened, they hide."

And I thought, *Where is there to hide?* It's not like a uterus has a supply closet. I looked down at my wife and she was fighting to stay awake so that she could witness the birth.

"I'm gonna be sick," she told me. The nurse handed me

one of those plastic hospital basins shaped like a kidney bean to place near her mouth and she drooled bile into it. She began crying, the tears pooling along the bottom ridge of her glasses' lenses.

"This is so awful, Drew."

"You're doing great. It's all gonna be over soon."

"It's horrible. I can feel them reaching in."

"It'll all be over soon and we'll have a beautiful son and you won't remember any of this. Not the waiting. Not the Cervidil. Not the monitors. Not even this hospital. Please, just hang on."

"I love you."

"I love you so much, just please hang on. I swear to you it'll be okay."

Dr. Kleinbaum yanked the baby out and held him over the curtain, like this was some kind of puppet show.

"You did it!" I screamed to my wife. "You fucking did it!"

She gave the baby a kiss. "I'm going to pass out now."

"By all means."

And pass out she did. Once the baby pops out, you assume that's the end of it, that they stitch Mommy up in five seconds and you go about your merry way. But in reality, a C-section is major surgery, which means layers upon layers of dermis and subcutaneous tissue must be repaired, the stitches made only after the placenta and the amniotic fluid have been removed. My wife slept in relative peace while I sat there, watching the silhouettes move ominously to and fro on the other side of the curtain and hearing the awful sounds of a medical vacuum sucking up the afterbirth.

"Are you guys almost done?" I asked.

"Not quite," said the doctor. "We have to massage her uterus back into place from the inside."

"Oh Jesus, don't tell me that."

I could see the doctor on the other side of the curtain laboring feverishly, as if he were mining for coal. Meanwhile, the baby was over in the corner of the room, having his vitals checked and his umbilical cord snipped (they don't allow the father to snip the umbilical after a Caesarian for reasons of sterilization). He was perfect—a real live being created out of virtually nothing. He was much better off than my wife or me, frankly. No mixed-up intestines for our second kid; only our third one would get to experience that particular thrill. They started to wheel him away to the nursery while my wife was still being stitched up. The nurse asked me if I wanted to leave her to go with my son, and suddenly I felt as if I was being torn between loyalties. My poor wife was still a piece of meat lying on a cold surgical table. But you only get to be there for the first few moments of the child's life once.

I went with the baby. I bathed him and changed him and swaddled him under a warm light in the nursery. Eventually, he fell asleep and the nurse encouraged me to go to the postpartum recovery room to do likewise.

I staggered out into the hallway. It was later in the morning now. My son happened to be born the day the president was being inaugurated. I dragged my body through the maternity ward as nurses and doctors and patients in wheelchairs gathered around every available TV set to watch the ceremony. I walked past all of it oblivious to the moment, like a caveman who had just woken up after being frozen in ice.

Inside the room, there was a little loveseat that pulled out for fathers to sleep on, and for thirty minutes I sank into a sleep so dark and black, I felt as if I could never be pulled out of it. There are many memorable things about watching a child being born, but what sticks with you the most is the exhaustion—the toll of the process, for both you and your wife (your wife more so), from conception all the way to delivery. It's the sense that you will never find yourself more physically or emotionally drained. It's almost as if God planned it that way. It's almost as if He designed it so that you won't be surprised when you find yourself running on empty for the next two decades.

EVENING AT THE IMPROV

The hardest part of giving a kid a bath is getting the kid *into* the bath. When my daughter was a baby, we could just throw her in the sink against her will and wash her like she was a saucepan. But as she learned to walk and talk and developed working muscles, getting her in the bath became more and more difficult. I had to find a way to get her to *want* to take a bath, which meant offering bribes or threatening punishment, often in tandem. *You'll get candy, or you'll never get candy again.*

Then, one night, I figured out a third technique. I went up to her while she was playing downstairs and told her the exciting news.

"Mommy bought you something at Target today!"

"She did?"

"Uh-huh. But it's upstairs. Let's go upstairs to see it!"

She flew up the stairs and I quickly closed the baby gate at the top of the steps behind her so that she couldn't get back down. The girl was three years old now, but the nuances of opening a baby gate were still a mystery to her. You had to push down on the tab while simultaneously lifting the gate up, and I deliberately used my body to shield my hand every time I opened it so that she wouldn't learn the technique. It was the only thing I still had over her.

"You closed the gate!" she wailed.

"I know. That's because it's . . . BATHTIME! BATH-TIME BATHTIME BATHTIME!"

"Noooooo! I don't wanna take a bath! You tricked me!"

She grabbed the bars on the gate and rattled them like a caged prisoner.

"Sweetheart, I tricked you because I love you," I said, "and because there's yogurt in your hair."

"Did Mom get me anything?"

"Oh, yeah, she got you some underwear."

"I DON'T LIKE UNDERWEAR!"

"Well, *I* thought the underwear was exciting. My mistake. Let's hop in the bath now."

"NO!"

"Umm . . . please?"

"NO!"

Then I had an idea.

"We could tell jokes," I said.

"Jokes?"

"Mmm-hmm. Remember that joke about the interrupting cow that you li—"

"MOO!"

"Yes, that one. You're very clever. Want to hear more?"

"Okay!"

"I'll tell you more, but only if you shake a tail feather and get in the tub."

She stripped down naked and bounded into the warm water. I soaped her up and told her the same tired knock-knock jokes a few times over. *Orange you glad I didn't say banana*, etc. But the material was wearing thin on her, and I had yet to wash her hair. You can take a child swimming and she won't complain for a second about getting water on her face. But get water on her face in the tub and she'll react like you just threw acid into her eyes.

"I have to wash your hair," I told her.

"I don't wanna wash my hair."

"I know you don't. But all you have to do is look up and the water won't get in your eyes. I swear this works and you never listen to me."

"No."

"How about this: Why don't *you* tell *me* a joke?"

"Me?"

"Yeah. Why should I have all the fun? You try one on me."

"Okay. Knock knock."

"Who's there?"

"Hairy."

"Hairy who?"

"Hairy eyeball."

Then she laughed so hard that her head naturally tilted

upward and I was able to wet her hair without any kind of fuss. I even managed to penetrate the dreaded outside shell of the hair. For some reason, the surface of a child's hair is virtually waterproof. One time, I poured water on the girl's hair and it all slid clean off, as if she had dunked her head in Thompson's WaterSeal. This time, I achieved full saturation down to the scalp.

"Oh, this is great!" I told her. "Tell another."

"Knock knock."

"Who's there?"

"Hairy."

"Hairy who?"

"Hairy eyeball in your butt."

More laughter. I snuck in a quick lather.

"You tell one, Daddy."

"Okay," I said. "Knock knock."

"Who's there?"

"Peanut."

"Peanut who?"

"A gallon of rotten peanut butter up your butt."

That was the killer. I could feel her laughter reverberating off the bathroom tile and now she was completely distracted. Jokes about butts WORKED. I could have washed her hair a dozen more times and not gotten a rise out of her.

"More!" she demanded.

Just like that, I had a meme. I scrambled to find more elaborate things to stick up another person's butt: toy ponies, a pint of vanilla ice cream, six corncobs, a milk truck. Eventually, I dropped the whole knock-knock formula and segued directly into singing Eddie Murphy's "Boogie in Your Butt" to her. She went nuts with laughter, throwing her head so far back I thought it might roll off her body. Right on cue, she started inventing her own lyrics.

"Put some gum in your butt!" she cried out.

I reacted with phony disgust and that made her laugh even harder.

"Put some ants in your butt!" I countered.

"Put a guitar in your butt."

"Put an astronaut in your butt."

"Put candy in your butt."

"Put Germany in your butt."

"What's Germany?"

"Well, whatever it is, it's in your butt now."

On and on we went. Everything we said was filthy and vile and horrible, but the bath itself was perfectly executed. She didn't splash water outside the tub once. She didn't bitch when I put the bath toys away or when I threw out the rubber duck that had black mildew leaking out of it. And when I opened the tub drain without her looking, she didn't immediately close it back up so that she could hang around in the bath for another eight hours, the way she usually did. The last of the bathwater swirled down the drain and she stepped out to receive her toweling like a civilized lady.

"That was excellent," I told her. "I've never had so much fun, and thank you for taking your bath without a fuss."

"Do one more!" she said.

So I found one more thing to stick up your butt and she slipped into her jammies without a fight.

"Let's go tell Mom!"

"No, no, no," I said. "She wouldn't get any of these jokes. Far too sophisticated for her. Let's just keep this between us for now. No butt talk outside the tub, all right?"

"All right."

And for the next six weeks, bathtime was the greatest time ever. I had found the key to bonding with my child in the tub, and all it required was me reciting a laundry list of terrifying rectal fillings: ham sandwiches, rice pudding, an eyeball coated in diarrhea, rabbit feet soaked in pee-pee, and such and such. Oh, we had a ball. I felt like I was holding court at the Comedy Cellar every night, bringing the house down with every set. It was magic.

Until . . .

"I overheard you in the bath," my wife said. "Why are you guys talking about putting stuff up butts?"

"It's just our special time."

"Drew."

"I didn't teach her any swearwords. Except for 'butt,' I guess. Does that count?"

" 'Put some barf salad up your butt'?"

"It's completely innocent."

"No more."

"I'll never have an audience like this again! Free speech, woman!"

"No more."

I relented. I knew I'd get caught eventually and I knew it was a cheap way of gaining my daughter's affections. I began to wonder how much damage all those butt jokes had done to her psyche. Now she was gonna head off to school and tell her teacher to stick a doodie fish pie up her butt and it would be all my fault. There was no going back now. The floodgates had been opened.

I brought her upstairs the next night and she jumped in the tub excitedly.

"Put some snowmen up your butt!"

"Right. About that . . . ," I began. "Listen, we can't make poopy jokes anymore."

"Why not?"

"Because it's just not right. I can't have you talking poopy talk once you get to school and all that. I'm sorry, girl. We can still tell jokes, but they gotta be clean."

"Hairy eyeballs?"

"I think that's allowable."

"Hairy cow eyeballs."

"Fish gut sandwich."

"Bucket filled with cow poop!"

"Let's make it cow tongues," I said. "No poop. We need to expand the repertoire."

"Oh, okay."

"Can I wash your hair?"

"Sure, Daddy."

"Thank you."

"And thank *you*, dead monkey ice cream sundae with monkey eyeballs on top."

FLATHEAD

D r. Ferris was unavailable for my son's six month appointment, which was too bad because Dr. Ferris was a master of his craft. He would walk into the office and it was like being greeted by a rock star. *He's here! At long last! Those two nurses who opened for him were okay, but now we've got the headliner!* The boy would stop crying and Dr. Ferris would grab his feet and play with him and call him all kinds of crazy nicknames and, in three seconds, develop a bond with him far stronger than the bond I had with the child. If I grabbed the boy's feet, he'd try to kick me in the nose. But when Dr. Ferris did it? MAGIC. Then he'd grab the shiny light thing doctors use and flash it in my son's ear and ask, "Is there a little birdie in this ear? I think there is! Chirp chirp!" and the boy would whoop and wail and the scene in the room would look like the cover of an AstraZeneca quarterly prospectus. Secretly, I was kind of jealous of Dr. Ferris. I didn't think I'd ever learn to be that good with children, not even my own. He also had fabulous hair. Dr. Ferris was good. Too good.

He was so good that his practice grew by the month, and getting appointments with him instead of one of his perfectly capable subordinates became more difficult. No one wants the B-lister at the doctor's office. They want the star attraction. They want to be special enough to have Dr. Ferris be the one checking on little Sally's vaginitis. But the man was unavailable one week when the boy needed a checkup, and so we had to settle for Dr. Dergan instead.

Dr. Dergan examined our son from head to toe, and we asked her all the usual questions. *Do you have some kind of magic way we can get him to sleep better? His shit looks like it has pearls in it. Is that okay? Where does he rank on the height and weight chart? Is he taller and heavier and therefore better than all the other kids?* Dr. Dergan answered our questions dutifully and then examined the boy's head.

"Hmm. Looks a little flat in the back."

"Excuse me?" I asked.

"Nothing alarming," she said. Doctors will never tell you any symptom is alarming unless there's an arrow sticking out of your chest. "Just a little bit flat. You might consider sending him to a specialist at Children's just to make sure."

She left, and my wife and I grabbed the boy's head, scrutinizing it obsessively.

"I guess it's kinda flat," I said. I took my hand and slid it up from the back of his neck to the top of his cranium. "See how it doesn't stick out after the neck? Maybe that's what she's talking about."

"I don't know. He looks fine to me," my wife said.

"Yeah. I mean, he has HAIR. The hair sticks out the back. You wouldn't even notice the back of his head."

"You don't think he has flat head syndrome, do you?"

We had heard about flat head syndrome, or plagiocephaly. Apparently, your baby can get a flat head if he lies down on his back for too long, which seems unfair since all babies lie down on their backs for hours and hours every day. Even worse, if you turn your baby's head to one side to prevent a flat head and you keep it on that one side for too long, his facial features are in danger of growing *into* that side, giving him a sideways face and making him look like a goddamn mutant. This was supposedly a real threat, even though I had never seen a grown adult with his face growing out of the side of his head like Man-E-Faces from the old *He-Man* cartoons.

We arrived home from the doctor's office with our son and I began freaking out that his head was misshapen and that I had no good method of preventing it, short of rotating him every five minutes like a chicken cooking on a spit. The doctor advised us to alternate between feeding him with our left hand and our right so that his muscles would grow in balance and he would be symmetrical. Ever try feeding a child with your nondominant hand? It feels like you're feeding him with a cadaver's hand.

I stared at my son and I thought back to the time when

I was waiting in line at a deli. The man in front of me was an attractive black man who happened to have the flattest head I had ever seen. It was stick straight in the back, and the crown of his head sloped up to it and formed a ridge at the back of his skull. He looked like a ski jump. I kept worrying that my son would grow up to be a ski jump.

"I still think he looks fine," my wife said.

"Maybe his head is deceiving us," I said. "Maybe it looks great to us because we're his parents and our brains have warped the image. Maybe to everyone else he looks like, you know, a griddle."

"I'm sure the neurologist will say he's okay and that'll be the end of it."

I kept running my hands along the boy's head, checking for imperfections as if I were a Third Reich phrenologist. I wanted to make sure there was adequate room for a fine brain that could perform math problems and come up with quick comebacks to dickish eighth graders. I put him down in the bouncy seat in the living room and my wife immediately chastised me.

"You can't put him down."

"I can't?"

"The doc says you should try to hold him a lot. It keeps the pressure off his head."

"But he's heavy."

"Just do it."

I took him out of the bouncy seat and held him, and held him, and held him. It's a fact that for every minute you hold a child, it triples in mass. By the tenth minute, I felt like I was holding up a truck. I had him against my body and the front of his onesie was soaked in my filthy chest sweat. I think he might have swallowed a chest hair.

"I can't hold this thing any longer," I told my wife.

"I'll take him."

"You'll have to hold him all day, because I have a bad back."

"Oh, that is so weak."

"What? It's true! I am medically endangering myself by holding that child aloft. And if I hold him for fifteen minutes and my spine breaks and you're left without Mr. Handsome Helper . . . Why, you're up shit creek, you are!"

My daughter walked into the room. "Can I hold him?"

"Oh, honey. That's very sweet of you," I said. "But, no, you'll drop him on his face."

"I looked up flat head syndrome online," my wife said to me. "Do you know how they fix it?"

"No."

"A helmet."

"Oh, no. Not a helmet."

"And they have to keep the helmet on for twenty-three hours a day."

"Really?"

"Really."

"Jesus."

When your child is in danger of having a flat head, you quickly learn that the money-grubbing executives at Big Helmet have gone to great lengths to make baby helmets seem like a normal, even fashionable thing. The helmets we looked up online were all designed to look like skateboarding equipment, decorated with skulls and guitars and diamonds, all kinds of KEWL and XTREEEM shit that will help a parent think, *This is cool and hip!* rather than, *GET THAT FUCKING HELMET OFF MY BABY.*

I looked at my son and thought about what a helmet would look like on him. I thought about all the looks he'd get. We live in an age of remarkable sensitivity, where other parents go to great lengths to appear tolerant and accepting of ALL children, not merely their own. But deep down, we're just as judgmental and catty a species as we were decades ago. The patina of niceness almost makes it worse. I thought about other parents looking at the boy—and he was such a beautiful, sensitive little boy—saying something nice about his race car helmet, and then going home and spitting out their real feelings. *That poor Magary boy, crawling around with a helmet on. I wonder if they'll have to tether him to a post in the yard.*

We drove the boy downtown to the big children's hospital and the lobby was filled with kids in wheelchairs, kids balding from chemo, and numerous other pale kids with sickly eyes. It was like being inside every public service announcement ever created. I wanted to cry my eyes out after taking three steps inside. The hospital itself was a masterpiece of health care industry bureaucracy. They had a main reception desk that sent you to another reception desk that sent you to a *third* reception desk. The elevator had a button for the third-and-a-half floor. I wanted to push it just to see if floor 3.5 contained a secret tunnel into the brain of John Malkovich.

After spending ages navigating the labyrinth, we arrived at the neurologist's office. He ran his fingers over my son's skull—just like a Third Reich phrenologist would!—and performed a series of mental tests on him. He snapped his fingers to one side of the boy's face and the boy's eyes followed. Ditto the opposite side. He checked the boy's ears. He pulled on the boy's arms. Then he turned to us.

"Well, his head *is* a bit flat in the back. But the good news is that his mental faculties seem just fine. He's not retarded or anything."

I swear, he used the word "retarded." I didn't even know retardation was on the table before he mentioned it.

"You might want to think about outfitting him in a helmet," he said.

"Does he really need one?" I asked.

"He's borderline. But you have to decide quickly because after a certain number of weeks, the bones set and the skull's shape is irreversible."

"But he wouldn't have to wear it for very long, right?"

"Actually, the general guideline is three to six months."

"Oh Jesus."

We left the doctor's office.

"Can you believe he actually said 'retarded'?" my wife asked me.

"I know! I wonder if he meant it medically. He seemed so casual about retardation."

"Do you think we should get the helmet?"

I had no idea. I looked at my son and his head looked fine to me. Two ears. Two eyes. A mouth. A chin. It was a perfectly acceptable head. I thought about what an incredible pain in the ass the helmet would be if we chose to buy one. Twenty-three hours a day. Several months. God knows if the boy would be able to sleep with that thing on. I pictured nights of endless screaming, with my wife reduced to tears, trying to soothe the baby while it was dressed like a linebacker. And the cost! Baby helmets cost hundreds of dollars. I didn't want the helmet because I didn't want to deal with all that bullshit, which is an awfully selfish thing to consider when deciding on the future shape of your progeny's skull. I imagined the boy turning thirty and having a ski jump head, all because I was too lazy and cheap and afraid of pitiful looks to strap a helmet on him for a few lousy months of his life, months that he wouldn't even end up remembering.

"I don't want to get him a helmet," I said.

"Neither do I," my wife said.

"He's got a nice head."

"He's got a *great* head."

"Yeah. What do doctors know about heads anyway?"

"I think we should check with Dr. Ferris, just to make sure."

So we did. We got an audience with the big man himself a week or so later. We plopped our son down in front of him and he proceeded to make the boy laugh louder than I had ever made him laugh. That stupid awesome Dr. Ferris.

"Does he need a helmet?" I asked.

He looked shocked by the idea. "What? A helmet? Nah," he said. "I almost never recommend the helmet. For the child to require a helmet, they have to be really . . ."

"Deformed?"

"The flatness has to be severe. I'm not sure a helmet's all that helpful anyway." He turned to my son. "Now who's a big bruiser? IS IT YOU?!"

The boy squealed with joy, and over the weeks and months his head grew. It grew up and down and out and to the side, in perfect proportion. Soon it was a perfect little sphere smothered in blond hair. No helmet necessary. I look at that head now, and all I think about is getting my co-pay from those first two appointments back. Baby helmets are a rotten lie.

DUI

An old friend was in town and wanted to go to a baseball game, which presented me with a rare chance to get away from the wife and kids for an evening. Any time I'm away from my family for an extended period of time, I lose any sense of common decency and become a vile repository for booze and meat. It's just ZOMG NO ONE WILL NOTICE ME EATING THIS FISTFUL OF BUTTERSCOTCH CHIPS. It's a grotesque transformation. One time, I was away on business and I ate three dinners in one night, just because I could. I didn't even enjoy the third dinner all that much. It was just piling on because I rarely had the chance to pile on, and piling on is fun, like when you empty the entire bottle of hotel shampoo onto your head.

I told my wife I was going out. Asked her, really.

"He's only gonna be here one night," I said. "It's a special occasion."

"That's fine," she said. "Just don't get too drunk."

"I won't."

"Seriously, don't get too drunk. Because then you wake up at three A.M. to barf in the toilet and that makes me wake up." My wife did not like having her sleep disrupted.

"Will you leave me alone? You can't get on my case for drinking too much before I've even had a chance to drink too much. Stop ruining my one night out, lady."

"Just keep it reasonable. Two, three drinks."

Now two or three drinks is a ridiculously low maximum, one I would surely surpass before the first inning. But I agreed to the limit anyway, even though I had no intention of holding myself to it. I figured that was one of those lies that came standard with a marriage. The wife tells the husband not to drink too much even though she knows he will, and the husband agrees even though he knows that she knows that he's gonna do fifty shots of Jameson the second he's out the door. It's like a running joke. *Good one, honey!*

"And try to come home at a reasonable hour," she said.

"I will."

I had a habit of pushing curfews. If I said I was gonna be home at ten, that usually meant I came home at eleven. A lot of times, I would call from the bar at ten to say I was "gonna be home soon" while trying to squeeze in one more drink. It wasn't because I wanted to stay away from home. I loved home. It was because I was out, and sometimes dads feel the urge to maximize the "freedom" because who the hell knows when you're gonna get another night out. Could be next week. Could be 2035. One time, I got home at 11:00 P.M. and my wife was dead asleep and I cursed myself for not staying out later since she wouldn't have noticed. *I could have spent another twenty minutes at the bar, staring at the TV! Dammit!*

So I went to the game to meet my old friend—along with a handful of others—and I drank. There was a rain delay, so we went to one of the stadium bars and I drank even more, staring out the windows and watching the entire span of the Anacostia River outside get pounded with fat raindrops. Each beer tasted better than the last. I had so much fun drinking during the rain delay that I was legitimately disappointed when play resumed and I had to take my seat again. *Why are we ruining this fun conversation by watching a baseball game?*

The game ended and we went to another bar and I drank more beer because the beer was still making me happy. Then I put in the obligatory phone call home.

"Where are you?" my wife asked.

"I'm coming home soon! Love you! Super love you!"

"Are you drunk? You're drunk."

"Drunk with LOVE."

"Just come home soon."

"I'll be right there. Honest."

I drank one more round before deciding that I had pushed the limits far enough. Fathers are like children in that they're always scheming to see exactly what they can get away with. I think a lot of men get married so that they'll have someone around to rebel against. Once you get out of school, there are no more parents or teachers to defy. Who's left? The old ball and chain.

Prior to the game, I had parked my car at the Metro station and taken the train into town. My reasoning was that this allowed me to drink all I pleased since I had such a short drive home. A mile, perhaps less. I was taking public transit 80 percent of the way to the stadium. Who gave a shit about the other 20 percent? It wasn't drinking and driving. It was drinking and *parking*. That's the kind of mentality you develop when you start habitually drinking and driving. You excuse your behavior at every possible turn because it *seems* so reasonable. You get comfortable with bullshitting yourself.

One of my friends offered to give me a ride from the bar downtown and I took her up on it. I told her to drop me at the Metro station and I'd take my car back home.

"I can just take you all the way home and you can get your car later," she said.

"Nah, nah," I said. "I want my car."

"Are you sure?"

"Yeah. I want my car." I didn't want to get up in the morning and explain to my wife that we had to drive back into town to fetch my car because I was too shitfaced to drive it home that night. Driving it home drunk was easier. Better.

Reluctantly, she took me back to my car and I hopped in, driving away drunk from the Metro garage like I'd done before. A few minutes later, the sirens flashed in my rearview.

• • •

The first time I ever got into a car with a drunk driver was when I was seventeen. I was working as a table runner at this Austrian restaurant up in northwest Connecticut. The head chef was a dictatorial bastard with a comical Teutonic accent. All the girl waiters had to wear tight dirndls, which was both demeaning and kind of hot. All the guy waiters had to wear black bow ties (clip-on) with white dress shirts and cheap black sneakers that became filthy by the end of every shift, with potatoes and other food scraps mashed into the treads. After the shift ended, the waiters and waitresses would pool their tip money together and go get shitfaced at one waiter's house. After working there a few weeks, I finally got invited to one of these after-parties. Once there, I drank so much that I threw up in my lap. I wiped myself off, returned to the party, and ended up in a car with four other people and a guy named Scott who was driving drunk back to his house. This was late at night, deep in the rural Connecticut woods, where the roads twist and turn and there are no streetlights or house lights anywhere and you feel like you're driving through some kind of endless black cloud.

I remember sitting in that car, asking myself why I was there, why I was bothering to endanger my life to sit in a car going nowhere I wanted to go. I'm sure any number of teenagers have died asking themselves the same question. It's such a stupid thing to do, to get into a car being driven by a blind-drunk person. And yet, when you're that age, you feel as if that's clearly the best option. You feel as if turning down the ride would be embarrassing, which is insane because the real shame is in being stupid enough to accept it. I easily could have died that night. We could have gone skidding off the road and that would have been that. Instead, we made it back to his house and I slept myself sober.

I'm sure there will be a moment in my children's future when they will be shitfaced at a party and someone who is equally shitfaced will entice them to take a ride in a car. And they'll have to decide, on a whim, whether that's a good idea. One stupid tiny moment in an ocean of hours and days and weeks and years, and maybe that's the moment when they'll randomly choose their own demise. You can do everything possible as a parent to prevent it, but ultimately, there are no guarantees. There never are.

The first time I ever got drunk and drove on my own was at another after-party for some other table-running job I had (the Austrian guy declined to bring me back the next summer, probably because I used to sing out loud while washing dishes). The head chef brought everyone to his house and cooked up food for us on three different grills, with buckets of One-Eyed Jack—a precursor to Mike's Hard Lemonade—dotted all over his lawn. I was eighteen, so I was at the proper age for consuming malt lemonade and thinking, *This tastes like candy!*

I drank one after another and quickly realized that I was shitfaced with no way home except my car. I could have called a cab. I could have gone with my tail between my legs to someone at the party, asking them for a ride home. I could have called my parents to pick me up. But there was a combination of laziness and that ever-present fear of embarrassment that prevented me from doing the right thing. Instead, I got into my car, drove back home, and blew a stop sign along the way. I was NOT driving the speed limit. I was halfway through the stop sign when I realized what I had done. I slammed on the brakes and skidded into the center of the intersection. No one was there. No one saw me do it. If another car had been around, I probably would have hit it. Maybe killed someone. Maybe died myself. After that, I promised myself I would never drink and drive again, but time has a way of loosening you up, of getting you to give bad ideas a second chance.

I began drinking and driving regularly after moving from New York to DC when I was twenty-seven. When you live in New York, you never drive, so going out and drinking is never a problem because there's always a cab or a subway or a bus or your own two feet to get you home. Anyone leaving New York for another American city has to find a way of adjusting to that new city's driving culture, taking your car with you virtually everywhere you go. I adjusted poorly.

One night in my new hometown, I was out with a friend, with no way home except for my car. I figured that one beer wouldn't impair me all THAT much, so I had a beer and drove home and everything was hunky-dory. So the next time I went out, I figured that perhaps TWO beers would be just fine. After all, one was no problem. Why not one more? In no time, I was merrily drinking and driving every weekend. I stopped counting drinks. I became convinced that I was good to drive no matter how much I drank. I drank and drove with my wife in the car. A handful of times, I had a couple of drinks and drove with my kids in the car, which was irresponsible but softened my temper when they were kicking my seat. At any kid function like a birthday party or a playdate where booze was served, I drank. Adults need alcohol in that situation. You stop hovering over your kid and have an easier time talking to other parents. *Oh, you're building a new basement? FASCINATING. Do you have any more of this Cabernet? It's awesome. GLUG GLUG GLUG.*

The longer you go drinking and driving without getting caught, the more you become convinced that you'll NEVER be caught. Getting caught becomes the domain of other, less professional drunk drivers: teenagers getting loaded on peach schnapps, hobos, athletes who drive too fast, etc. Not you. You wildly underestimate how much the alcohol impairs your abilities behind the wheel. *I'm okay to drive.* I said that a lot, as if my own bullshit assessment mattered.

In the back of my head, I knew it was wrong. There were nights when I would wake up at 3:00 A.M. to go piss and to down a glass of water and two Advil to prevent a hangover the next morning. And while standing in my bathroom, with nothing but the moonlight illuminating my bloated body, I would think to myself, *Why did I drink and drive like that? What am I, stupid?* In that moment, I would feel a tremendous surge of dark guilt and shame, a sense that I had endangered the welfare of my wife and children for no good reason. It was that sickening feeling you get when you know you've done the indefensible.

Then the morning would come and I would forget all

about it. Despite the occasional self-induced guilt trip, I came to *enjoy* drinking and driving. Sometimes I would go out and look forward to the drive home more than the actual time spent at the bar. I loved the feeling of the car zooming along when I was buzzed. Sometimes I would blast the music and take curves at a decent speed, pretending I was driving an Alfa Romeo with a cadre of Russian spies hot on my ass.

One spring day, I met some friends after work at a bar to watch basketball and I drank five or six beers. Then I drove home on the Beltway—one of the worst roads in America— and got stuck in traffic. But I couldn't have cared less about sitting there in that jam. I reveled in being the only person stuck on the road that had no problem with it. I rolled down the window, took in some fresh exhaust, and sang along to the radio without a care in the world. I was having a blast, alone, drunk in my car.

The second I knew I was gonna be arrested, I accepted it. There was no frantic search for a penny to suck on or some wild deliberation in my own mind about taking a Breathalyzer. I sat there calmly and waited for my fate to be sealed. Officer Burgess had me step out of the car, walk the line, say the alphabet backward, run an obstacle course, do burpees, and all that other fun stuff. Cops don't do this to figure out if you're drunk. They know that the second you roll your window down. I think they do this just for fun, and I can't blame them. It really builds up the anticipation for administering the Breathalyzer and putting on the cuffs.

"Close your eyes," he ordered.

"Okay."

"Now touch your nose."

I felt my finger touch the point of my nose and I had to suppress my glee. Maybe I was getting away with it.

"Okay, Mr. Magary, I'm gonna have you take a Breathalyzer test."

Shit.

He led me over to the Breathalyzer and had me blow. Seconds later, he took my hands behind my back and I felt the cuffs go on. They were cool to the touch.

"I'm going to book you for DUI, Mr. Magary."

"What did the Breathalyzer say?"

"I can't tell you that right now."

"Really?" It seemed like such a tease.

"Sorry."

He helped me into the front seat of his car. I wondered why I didn't get the backseat treatment. *What if I try to bite his penis off while he's driving me to the station? There's nothing stopping me, except for common sense and basic human decency.* I made small talk with the officer, as if we were on a business trip together. "Busy night?" I asked. What a fucking stupid question.

I stared out the window and thought about the impending fallout of my arrest. My wife would be angry, to be certain. I might go to jail. I was gonna have to cough up a lot of money that I would rather not cough up. I dreaded the idea of not being able to drink for a while. I remember feeling like the party was over, that life was going to stop being fun now. Somehow I had become so fucked in the head that driving a car after a few beers was now an important facet of my existence, something I didn't want to end. I was a suburban dad with two kids. *Lemme have my one last piece of rebellion. Pathetic, meaningless rebellion.*

Once Officer Burgess took me into the station, he cuffed me to a table that had a special steel bar running underneath that served as a prisoner hitching post. Then he had me fill out reams of paperwork and snapped a Polaroid of me.

"Is that my mug shot?" I asked. I kinda wanted one. You know, for posterity.

"No," he said. "I just take this so I can remember your face when I see you in court."

He morphed into my DUI field guide, telling me everything that was going to happen to me and explaining that I needed a ride home since my license was now temporarily suspended. He also recommended a handful of state-approved alcohol education classes, which you must take prior to showing up in court.

"You think I'll be able to manage this without a lawyer?" I asked. I already knew the answer.

He shook his head with genuine regret. "It's unlikely, Mr. Magary. You can try, but I wouldn't advise it. I'm sorry." I visualized pretty whirlwinds of cash streaming out of my shorts pocket.

After hours of being processed, Officer Burgess handed me my paperwork, which included my official BAC of .10, and I was formally released. My friend picked me up at the station and drove me to my house. Just as we were turning the corner onto my street, my phone rang and I saw the word "HOME" flashing on the screen. And now the shame and regret and sadness arrived in a rising tide. *Why? Why, why, why?* I took my wife's call and told her as fast as I could, like ripping off a Band-Aid to get the pain over with.

I walked through the door and she greeted me at the top of the stairs, exhausted. It was now 3:00 A.M.

"I thought you might be dead," she said.

"I'm so sorry."

"We can talk about it later. I just want sleep."

The next day, she barely spoke to me. I wasn't her husband that day. I was just this *thing* that she had to deal with. For a single twenty-four-hour stretch, I felt convinced that my wife didn't love me anymore. Whatever life force is created when two people love each other had vaporized, and I could feel it. You could have strapped me to a table and sawed through my bones and it wouldn't have been as painful. Being unloved is like being homeless. Destitute.

My daughter was playing outside on the swing when my wife finally pulled me aside to unload. She didn't raise her voice.

"I'm hurt, and I'm angry."

I broke down in front of her. "Please forgive me. Please. It'll never happen again. Please believe me." I kept saying that line over and over again. *Please believe me.* I thought if I said it enough, maybe it would stick. It began to grate on her.

"Stop saying that. I'm not gonna believe you right now. You have to actually not do it again."

Wives aren't dumb. They aren't just going to absolve

you on the spot. You'd never learn your lesson that way. If forgiveness were that swift, it wouldn't be worth anything. That's the hardest part of being married—when you've fucked up and want desperately to mend everything quickly, only your partner won't give you the satisfaction.

The drunk driving wasn't even the worst part of it. As a result of my arrest, I had my license suspended, making her the sole family driver for two months. She was far more pissed about that than the actual drunken driving, and I couldn't blame her. In a family of four or more, it's crucial to have at least two functioning drivers. A parent that can't drive isn't a parent at all. It's an old dog that should be dragged out and shot.

My daughter continued playing as I cried to my wife for absolution. Later on, I told the girl that I was going to have to go to class for a few nights.

"What kind of class?" she asked.

"Uh . . . a learning class," I said. "Here, have a pretzel."

I walked into alcohol education class and was greeted by the sight of twenty other drunk drivers sitting in a loose circle: rich, poor, black, white, Hispanic. It was a Rainbow Coalition of fuckups, almost heartwarming in a way.

The multitude of DUI arrests in this country has created a microeconomy of lawyers, alcohol education facilities, and local government agencies. Your arrest helps keep the industry afloat, and nowhere is that more apparent than in alcohol education. No one in my class seemed at all remorseful about getting arrested. In fact, many of them felt dicked over by the system for having the gall to catch them drinking and driving when everyone else did it anyway. The class was just like detention, only sadder.

Class started at 7:00 P.M. every night, which further infuriated my wife because 7:00 P.M. was right around kiddie put-down time, when it's crucial for all hands to be on deck to deal with bathing, brushing teeth, and threatening the kids with prison for coming downstairs more than six times after being tucked in. Before the teacher arrived, we would sit in a circle and make small talk, which always revolved around three questions:

1. How did you get arrested?
2. What was your BAC?
3. How many classes you got left?

Everyone sympathized with everyone else, and everyone thought everyone else's arrest was some serious bullshit. There was an immigrant who got arrested for being drunk in a parked car. There was a twitchy, dark-haired man who was bitter because he had to travel all the way from Virginia each week for class. There was a seventeen-year-old high school student who was now grounded until 2027. Everyone complained about lawyer fees, about the cops, and about the obligations of the class. My first night in class, a girl asked me where I got pulled over.

"On Rockville Pike," I said.

"Oh my God, was Officer Burgess the one who got you?"

"Yeah, that was his name."

"He got me too!"

Suddenly, we had so much in common. It was like we were siblings. Officer Burgess was the Scourge of Rockville Pike.

"What was your BAC?" she asked me.

"Point one-oh," I said.

A handful of other students let out winces because the legal limit is Maryland is .08. I was THIS close to not being too drunk, even though that doesn't really mean anything. I was plenty drunk. We all revealed our BACs to each other: .09, .16, .18, .25. I tried to form a mental picture of what each level of drunkenness looked like. I was delighted at how many students had higher BACs than me. It made me feel like less of a criminal.

Every week, a handful of students would announce that they had just one or two classes left to go before being freed, and the rest of the class would congratulate them despite also being deeply jealous of them. New arrestees would come in to take the veterans' place in class. They are never short on students in alcohol education.

Once the teacher arrived and we had all settled in, she would have us say our names and then ask us if we had "used" in the past week. The correct answer to this was obviously NO, even if you had drunk alcohol in the past week (I abstained for eight months after I got arrested). But more than a handful of students would happily confess and then watch the teacher scribble down the answer without realizing that she was there to report such things to the courts.

One lady even showed up to class drunk, as if she had been shotgunning beers on the Metrobus ride over. The teacher asked her if she had used the past week and she was like, "Of course! But what's the big fucking deal? AM I RIGHT, GUYS?!" A lot of scribbling after that. I was so embarrassed for her, I wanted to gag her and hide her in the closet so she wouldn't dig a deeper hole for herself. *You fool! Don't you understand that the teacher is a government mole?!*

The teacher's only job was to press play on a DVD player so that we could watch the educational video for the night. Most of the time, this consisted of an episode of A&E's *Intervention*, which was a fantastic show, and part of me was happy to be arrested just so I could discover it. We also watched *Leaving Las Vegas* over the course of three classes, because there's no better lesson for alcoholics than to watch a dying, insufferable drunk manage to score with a smoking-hot prostitute.

Despite its flaws, alcohol education was uniquely successful at shaming me, at making me feel like a total fucking loser. Everyone who shows up to a DUI class thinks that they don't belong there and that they're better than everyone else in the room. It's like walking into an OTB parlor by accident. *These people are degenerates. I'm the anomaly.* That's the standard alkie train of thought. But down in my guts, I knew that I belonged in that class. I wasn't there by accident. I was just as stupid and irresponsible as the rest of them. And it's never comforting to feel like a stupid person. You wanna die from embarrassment. That's the real deterrent to a second DUI arrest. Not the money. Not the inconvenience. It's the self-ridicule.

The alcohol education course also required students to attend AA once a week for eight weeks. The teacher handed me a green booklet of meetings that took place around the area, and I perused it like a college student going over a course catalog. There were AA classes for people of all stripes: vegans, dog owners, evangelicals, pastry chefs, you name it. I chose one called "We Agnostics" because it promised a secular approach to sobriety, and I wanted to avoid prayer circles if I could. The meetings were held in a church, which kinda defeated the purpose of the enterprise, but I went anyway.

My first night there was in August. There was no air-conditioning and the opening speaker was an elderly man who wore open-toed shoes despite having hideous, gnarled old-man feet. I tried desperately to avoid staring at them, but they reached into my line of vision, following me everywhere I went. For reasons I didn't understand, he spent half an hour talking about his wife nearly getting hit by a bus. And while I sympathized with him for having a wife who nearly got hit by a bus, I really wanted him to get to the fucking point. I began to worry that AA was less a refuge for alcoholics than for lonely people. *Is this all people do here? They come here to bore other people with tedious bullshit?*

But then he began to talk about his addiction. His intervention was on a beach. His wife and daughter were the only attendees. Whenever he traveled, he had to look up the nearest meeting because he didn't want to fall back into the hole, to ruin the effort his family had put into saving him by the ocean. Other people soon chimed in, and everything about AA began to make sense. Many of the alcohol education students despised the AA requirement because it further inconvenienced them, and I saw more than a few of them sign the attendance sheet passed around in every AA meeting and then get up to leave halfway through. But I didn't because it seemed like a huge insult to the people who CHOSE to be there, the people who went to AA because they knew they would die if they didn't.

One night, after a woman in the meeting asked me who I was and why I was there, I told everyone about my arrest. I told them about the nights when I would get loaded and happily drive home.

"I don't know why I liked doing that," I told them.

There was another old man in our meetings, a man who came to each meeting wearing a finely tailored business suit. He turned to me and spoke slowly, in small sips.

"I'm glad you're here tonight, Drew," he said. "Because you're not alone. I've been an alcoholic for forty years. My parents were alcoholics. My grandparents were alcoholics. My four brothers are alcoholics. I have a disease. And I know that, one day, this disease will kill me." The way he said that last sentence, I didn't doubt him in the slightest. "And I *loved* drinking and driving. Adored it. Lived for it. I can't drive by a liquor store on the way home now because if I do, I'll pull over and drink and drive on the way home. I know I will. I want to do it as much as I ever have. This meeting . . . this is what's keeping me alive, keeping me breathing. So I'm glad you're here."

"I'm not gonna lie to you," I told him. "When I've done the required amount of AA meetings, I don't know that I'll be back here. I'm not ready to brand myself an alcoholic, even if I know that's a typical sign of denial. I made a terrible mistake and I want to learn from it. And I promise you, if it happens again, I will be here, and it won't be because the court ordered me here. It'll be because I *know*. I'll be ready to say to you that I'm definitely an alcoholic, and that I don't have the power to stop it."

"Well, good luck to you, Drew," he said. "I hope you never have to come back. I hope you don't have what I have."

The difference in attitudes between the people at the AA meeting and the malcontents in the alcohol education class epitomized the struggle that went on inside my own head. You have to fight your own cynicism. You have to shut up that little voice in your head that tells you, *This is not a big deal.* It's easy to listen to that voice because so many people drink and drive and so many people get away with it. It's easier to tell the problem to fuck off than it is to try to fix it. But you have to acknowledge your massive failure as a human being and work to correct it because otherwise—what was the fucking point? What was the point of spending thousands on lawyer fees and being cuffed and hauled into a police cruiser if you're not gonna learn anything from it?

Whenever something lousy happens, my wife likes to say that it happens for a reason, but that's only true if you *give* the event meaning. It's up to you to make it the catalyst for something good, something better. I came to view my DUI arrest as a purchase. I was buying the sordid thrill of being arrested, the joy of discovering a very good reality show, the experience of standing before a judge in pants-shitting fear, and the wisdom of listening to real people struggling with an addiction that many of them knew, deep down, would eventually defeat them. That had to be worth my four thousand dollars. I wasn't going to just piss my money away and not get anything out of it. Oh, and I wasn't gonna drink and drive ever again. And I haven't.

My lawyer was a short man with a gimpy leg who resided in a suburban office that looked like a hoarder's fruit cellar. There was paper everywhere, stacked to the ceiling: briefs, depositions, sworn affidavits, notes scrawled in longhand on garish yellow legal pads. Only he knew where everything was and why it was there. He gave me a "discount" on my defense, a bargain basement price of $1,800. (I was charged another $2,200 in fines and alcohol ed tuition.)

He brought me in front of the judge and I quickly realized that the only reason people hire lawyers is so that their case isn't called last on the docket. One of the guys in my alcohol education class navigated the system without a lawyer and ended up paying a *smaller* fine than I did, which I thought was bullshit. The judge called on me to stand up and enter my plea to a reduced charge, and then asked if I had anything to say to the court. I had to strangle myself

SOMEONE COULD GET HURT

from being Mr. Dramatic and subjecting the court to a very long speech that would no doubt win me an Academy Award. The judge looked like a man who heard those speeches once every forty minutes and hated them with every cell of his beating heart. Before my turn, I had seen a wealthy suburban dad break down and apologize profusely before the court and the judge looked as if he were being handed a soiled diaper.

"Do you have anything you'd like to say to the court, Mr. Magary?" the judge asked.

"No, sir. No."

He banged his gavel and I went downstairs to get my paperwork processed. All the fines had to be paid by money order. The court system, shockingly, does not trust checks that come from convicted criminals.

For the final portion of my DUI penance, they sent me to a lecture for all DUI offenders at a local vocational school. The auditorium had two thousand seats, and for this lecture, every seat was taken. I was forced to stand with dozens of others in the back. They arrested three people for showing up drunk to the lecture and violating the terms of their probation. Policemen walked right up to them during the talk and escorted them out. The man next to me thought the drunks were planted as a scare tactic. In my case, the tactic succeeded. I was terrified.

Our lecturer was a local man who had lost his daughter in an accident when she took a ride with a drunk driver— the same kind of pointless, late-night ride I took back in

Connecticut fifteen years earlier. One year later, her best friend was also killed by a drunk driver in the exact same spot where *she* had been killed.

"I don't really care about what happens to you people," he told us. "I'm just here so I can talk about my daughter. This is how I keep her alive."

He passed around her picture and made us say her name out loud. The picture came to me and I stared it. I thought about every picture ever taken of my daughter, and how it could be me passing her image around to a bunch of fucking lowlifes who would probably never get the hint. Then I thought about that Polaroid that Officer Burgess took of me when I was first caught. He never did show me that picture. I wonder what I look like. I wonder if I look dumb. I bet I do. I bet I look dazed. I bet I look almost offensively casual about the proceedings, someone so out-of-touch with what's right and what's wrong that he can't see the damage he's doing. I wonder if I look any different today. I pray to Christ that I do.

SPINNING WHEEL OF DEATH

It was Saturday and my parents were in town and we needed something to do. This happened every weekend, with my wife and me feverishly racking our brains to figure out a decent place to take the children. We couldn't just keep them in the house all day. If we did that, everyone would kill each other by 3:00 P.M. We had to find some new and dazzling adventure to take them on. This is why apple orchards make zillions of dollars. My wife was going out with friends that afternoon. It was up to me and my folks to divert the little ones.

"You guys could take the kids to the Baltimore aquarium," my wife suggested.

"How much does it cost?" I asked.

We hopped online and the admission fee was $28 per person. Kids were NOT free, which was bullshit. I immediately pictured plunking down $112 and watching my kids demand to leave after five minutes of staring at clown fish.

"That can't be right," I said. "Twenty-eight bucks? That's insane. Who can pay that?"

"Jenny down the street got a family membership. They go all the time."

"What does that cost?"

"A hundred fifty, I think."

"JEEEEEESUS. Is that per person?"

"I'm not sure."

"Why does everything have to cost something? This is crap."

I always had a hard time coming up with an excursion that was new and interesting and didn't cost irritating amounts of money. In the end, we usually succumbed to wandering aimlessly around a mall, or going to a movie, or attempting (and failing) to eat lunch at a modestly priced restaurant. I looked up movie listings and there was nothing bland and shitty enough to be appropriate for little children.

"You could just stay here and do a craft project," my wife said.

"No way." I wasn't the kind of parent who could come up with brilliant craft projects for my children to do for five hours straight. Family magazines are littered with these ideas. MAKE A PIRATE BOAT OUT OF OLD MILK CARTONS! No fucking way. I wasn't gonna sit at the dining room table for that long cutting out pictures of parrots and getting dabs of Elmer's glue on my elbows.

"Oh, let's just take them to the playground," my mom suggested. So we did.

I have a vision in my head of what the perfect playground is like. It rests on a twelve-inch-thick cushion of mulch— that soft, recycled tire mulch that would be fun to jump on while stoned. And the dream playground equipment is never wet from rain or morning dew, because dew ruins everything. There are swings—many of them, including big kid swings, baby swings with nice wide foot holes that never trap baby shoes, and none of those evil plastic yellow swings that are meant for handicapped kids but are often occupied by fat, tired parents looking for a place to sit. The swings at my dream playground swing themselves so that I don't tire out after five seconds of pushing my kid high enough to kick the clouds. And there are enough swings to go around so that I don't have to worry about other shithead parents being oblivious and letting their kid hog the swing for eight hours straight. You can try to stand with your kid near these parents and get them to overhear you saying, "Now, Johnny, as soon as this nice young lad is off the swing, you'll get your turn," and it won't matter. Those people never seem to take your subtle cue. They're off in Shitheadland, never to return.

Our playground for the day was not my dream playground. Much more of a Shitheadland playground. It had four swings, which wasn't much but at least gave it Real Playground status. But it had many other unwelcome hazards. There was a merry-go-round, which was not a carousel but rather a giant metal plate with handles that kids used to subject each other to gravitational forces of up to 5 Gs. There was a play structure that rose up ten feet in the air, with wide openings along the barriers that allowed for toddlers to fall to their death at any moment. The structure was labeled for kids five to twelve. *Well, what am I supposed to do with a two-year-old, Mr. Playground Designer? Have him build mud huts over to the side?*

To get to the playground, we had to walk along a busy street and cross under a filthy highway overpass. My daughter, now five, took her bike and blasted ahead of us, with me shouting at her to stay on the innermost portion of the sidewalk so that a bus driver wouldn't run her down. She didn't listen to me, but I kept shouting at her anyway because my parents were there and I wanted them to feel like I had control of the situation. My son, now two, trailed behind her on a tricycle. I occasionally used my foot to guide him away from the road, like a shopping cart with a bad wheel.

The entrance to the playground was blocked by a series of bikes and scooters lying on the ground. I cleared them out of the way so that my kids could run through. Then I looked around for the children who'd left their bikes lying around so that I could murder them with my icy stare. No such luck. My parents and I took to a nearby bench that was already capable of causing third-degree burns because the entire playground was exposed to the sun. My daughter went running onto a rope bridge. My son followed her and immediately got his feet tangled in the ropes and was stuck on the bridge, crying. I assume the rope bridge was added to the playground at the last moment by some kind of giant spider goddess who needed a surefire trap for luring human children.

I untangled my son and returned to my spot on the bench next to my folks, who offered a running analysis of the children as they watched them in action.

"She plays so well by herself," my mom said of the girl.

"Thanks, Mom."

"She's very tactile, you know? She's very interested in the texture of things. Maybe she'll be a designer. And I love how her hair bounces."

"That *is* a great head of hair," my dad agreed.

Ten minutes after we arrived, a middle-aged mother showed up at the playground dressed like a Turkish hooker. She had long black hair and was wearing a tight blue tank with painted-on skinny capris and platform shoes that sank down three inches into the mulch. I'm certain that she had a speed dating session set up at the local Romano's Macaroni Grill at happy hour.

This woman was clearly violating protocol by not wearing yoga pants and a hoodie to the playground. But I didn't say anything because that wasn't my business. She kept chasing her kid around in her giant platform shoes in front of us, and I tried not to stare at her even though her outfit was basically a giant sandwich board that said "STARE AT ME" in block letters. I kept it to myself, which would have worked out splendidly if my parents hadn't been sitting next to me.

My parents live in a very quiet part of northwest

Connecticut, the kind of place where you can go weeks on end without seeing another live body. Spotting a provocatively dressed human being counts as a real event for them, and so they began a running commentary on Turkish Hooker while I was trying to ignore her and make sure my son didn't get tangled up in the rope bridge for the ninth time.

"Look at that woman, Drew," my mom said.

"What? What woman?"

"That woman right there. Boy, she's heading out tonight."

"Oh Christ. She can hear you, Mom."

"Nonsense. Look at those pants. How do you get pants like that on?"

Meanwhile, the surface temperature of the playground was rising to roughly a million degrees, and I had lost track of my son. I scanned for him, but Turkish Hooker kept flouncing around in front of us, running her fingers through her hair like she was on the set of a goddamn L'Oréal ad. I stood up in a panic because any time I lose sight of my children at a playground I assume some deranged pederast has grabbed them and thrown them into a windowless van.

Then I realized my son was sitting in the tunnel slide, only he couldn't exit the tunnel slide because a ten-year-old was hanging out at the bottom of it, like a complete dick. Downward sliders should always have the right-of-way, but there are any number of older kids who have no respect for matters of slide etiquette. I spotted my son's shadowy lump through the opaque plastic and reassured him.

"Don't worry, son. You'll be able to get out once this

nice boy moves out of the way." I said the last sentence extra loud so that the ten-year-old would take the hint. I fully expected him to tell me to go fuck myself because ten-year-olds do that sort of thing. Instead, he got up immediately.

"Sorry about that."

"Oh, no problem," I said. "Thank you for moving."

And I was heartened for a moment. A playground, when you think about it, is something of a miracle. There are any number of opportunities for children to inflict fatal harm upon other children they don't know. They can push each other off structures. They can punch each other. They can strangle each other with swing chains. But that rarely happens, and when the ten-year-old made way for my son, I found myself marveling at how all these tiny, immature people were able to coexist in this spot in relative peace.

Then I noticed my daughter had made a new friend and that the new friend's dad was actively playing with both of them, which made me look terrible because I wasn't interacting with my daughter at all. This happens at playgrounds. If one parent does something, you follow his cue like a sheep. If she checks her phone, you check your phone. If he starts clapping and saying "YAY" while swinging his kid, you do the same. I wanted to have an equal presence in this impromptu playdate, only I had to keep an eye on my son and another eye on Turkish Hooker because my parents were demanding that I stare at her. Then I spotted a rumpled man walking around the playground with no child and I quietly feared that he was a serial killer hunting for victims. I needed six eyes in my head to keep tabs on everything.

My daughter ended up on the dreaded merry-go-round, which was now loaded with older kids. One twelve-year-old was spinning it using every last ounce of strength, like he was spinning the showcase wheel on *The Price Is Right*. There was another shithead kid wearing a tie-dyed shirt leaning off the side of the merry-go-round and deliberately allowing his own head to drag around on the mulch. There was no parent for this child anywhere in sight. The kid was clearly an orphan who had been left there to sleep under the climbing wall and forage for wild berries. His empty head doubled as a spinning weapon for any small child trying to approach the ride. I saw one kid try to grab the spinning wheel of death and she nearly had her arm torn out of the socket thanks to the centrifugal forces at work. Suddenly, my warm and fuzzy feelings about the playground being a utopia of cooperation faded away. I had to save my daughter from the merry-go-round before it came off its moorings and went flying off to the goddamn moon. I tried to address all the kids on the merry-go-round en masse.

"Let's slow this wheel down, guys," I said. "Someone could get hurt."

Again, a small miracle. A big kid hopped off and dug in his heels, and my daughter and a bunch of other kids went streaming from it, with a new batch of youngsters ready to hop on to be terrorized. The playground community had come through for me once more, and I relaxed.

But then my son came running to me. He had gone down the tunnel slide again and now he was crying. I assumed he had bumped his head on something because my son rammed his face into things fifty times a day. I bent down to hug him and reassure him, and I suddenly felt something warm and gooey on his ass. Terrified he'd diarrheaed all over himself, I turned him around and was confronted with a giant blob of . . . something. To this day, I don't know what it was. It was yellow. And it looked like pudding. I think it was banana pudding. I thought about tasting it to confirm (and because I really like banana pudding) but reconsidered. It could have been rat poison, or animal ejaculate, or any number of other unpleasant things that were not banana pudding.

"What the hell is this?!" I asked.

"Tunnow sly!" he said through tears.

"This was on the tunnel slide?!"

"Mmm-hmm. Tunnow sly."

"WHO PUTS FOOD ON THE TUNNEL SLIDE?!"

I went over to the tunnel slide, and it was clear that some piece-of-shit kid had smeared food all over it. Two other parents saw the crime but couldn't point the offending kid out. Maybe the ten-year-old who had been so nice before had laid a trap. Maybe it was one of the punks who left their scooters in the pathway. I looked around for any child who had trace evidence of banana pudding on his hands, and I daydreamed about pinning that child down and choking him to death for daring to infect my son with Pudding Butt. I searched high and low for the perpetrator, but Turkish Hooker kept getting in the way. And I could STILL hear my parents talking about her outfit from the bench a few feet away.

"You think she wears those shoes all the time?"

Then my daughter started screaming because she had blisters on her hands from attempting to cross the spinning monkey bars. My daughter was already proficient enough at normal monkey bars to gain entrance into any Afghan terrorist training academy. But this playground threw in the wrinkle of having circular monkey bars that were set on an angle and could spin around. No mortal child can cross these monkey bars. You have to be a full-grown silverback gorilla if you want to navigate these bars properly. They should have installed a pit of alligators beneath the bars just to add a dash of excitement.

Now my daughter had stigmata on her hands and my son had pudding dripping from his shorts and I had no emergency pants and undies for him because I'd forgotten them, along with a bottle of water and bunny crackers to snack on. Finally, I lost my shit.

"No more!" I said. "We're leaving!"

I began walking away from the playground, with my son trailing behind, riding a tricycle in just his underwear, and my daughter asking me to carry her thirty-pound bike all the way home because her hands hurt. I carried my son's shorts between my thumb and index finger so that none of the animal ejaculate would get on my hands.

We managed to trudge all the way back home. The children slumped in front of the TV like dying soldiers and I took off my shoes and socks and sat in my recliner and wriggled my toes and that little moment—that split second of relief—made the entire enterprise worth it.

My mom sat down next to me.

"That was a wonderful time!" she said.

"Yeah, it was great," I said.

"I loved how both kids interacted with the other kids. They're very social, you know."

"That they are."

"But did you SEE that woman? She was one hot ticket!"

"YES, I SAW HER, MOM."

FAKA

I was on the phone with my dad and he happened to be home alone, which meant that he was more eager than usual to talk about whatever was on his mind. Window replacement was among the favored topics. We were five minutes into the conversation when my daughter started yelling at me from the stairs. Children HATE it when you talk on the phone to other people. When you're a parent, every conversation is a half conversation. I have conversations from five years ago that still need to be picked up. My wife was out running an errand, so I was the only one around for her to badger.

"DAD!"

I ignored her and kept talking to my father. "That's what I told her! You don't have to replace the windows. They just need a good strip job—"

"DAD! DADDDDDDDDY!"

"Oh god dammit. Dad, can I call you back?"

"So that's it?" my dad said. "You're just gonna hang up on me and go do her bidding?"

It takes virtually nothing for your parents to get under your skin. My dad asked that one simple question and I could infer pages upon pages of subtext. *You're a pussy because you're doing whatever your kids tell you to do. When I was raising you, we never gave in to you kids like that. Your generation is weak and you are an overly permissive slave to your offspring. You should hush that child up and teach her some goddamn manners.* All of that was packed into the question. And the amazing thing was that I fell for it. Immediately. One question altered my entire parenting philosophy right there, on the spot. I was now torn between dealing with the girl and looking bad in front of my dad when he wasn't even in the house.

"Sweetheart," I told my daughter, "I'm talking to Papa on the phone. I'll be right with you."

"I wanna talk to you NOW!"

Then I got really stern because I knew my old man was listening. "Young lady, you sit there and you be quiet until I'm finished."

She did neither of those things. Instead, she screamed at me. No words, just a piercing scream that blew my Eustachian tubes apart. She held out her hand like it was a claw, like she wanted to rake my face off. Then she screamed again, as if she had experienced some kind of trauma that only allowed her to communicate through primal wails. Now I was fucking livid.

"Dad, I have to deal with this," I said. I wanted to emphasize that I was hanging up on him strictly so I could put my daughter in her place.

I stormed up to her. "WHAT? What is it that's so important that you have to scream?"

She screamed again. The screams had successfully gotten me to direct all of my attention toward her. The fact that it was negative attention—white-hot, furious attention—didn't matter to her. Kids don't give a shit. They're little trolls. If they've riled you up, they've done their job.

"Young lady, I want you to go to your room."

"NO! You go to YOUR room!"

"I'm going to count to three."

"Faka."

"What?"

"Faka." And then she laughed.

"What is faka? Are you trying to say . . . Well, I can't say what I think you're trying to say—"

"Faka."

"Stop saying that. That sounds like a bad word and I don't like you using bad words."

"Faka."

"Okay, that's it. NO DESSERT."

"I hate you!" she screamed.

"Okay, no dessert for two nights."

"ROAR!"

"A week."

"Faka."

"A month."

"Faka."

"NO DESSERT EVER AGAIN. THAT IS THE END OF DESSERT. Kiss all the cupcakes and lollipops good-bye, missy. Because as of today, they are gone FOREVER."

She screamed again and I snapped. I picked her up and she thrashed against me, all elbows and knees. She wasn't light. I could feel my back acting up, and now I was pissed at her for making my back hurt even though I was the one who'd made the stupid decision to pick up a thrashing child. I bounded up the stairs with her to her room and put her on the floor. Then I walked out and locked the door from the outside (I'd switched the locks on the door specifically for this purpose, which is probably a violation of eight different fire codes). I started back down the stairs and she immediately began banging on the door, screaming her head off. Her rage seemed limitless, as if she could keep at it for days without needing sleep or food or air. Children will always have more stamina than you. I expected the door to come flying off its hinges at any moment. My son came up from the basement.

"Deddy, wud going on?" he asked.

"Stay there. Don't go near your sister right now."

Then my daughter somehow managed to scream even louder, as if summoning a bullhorn from down inside her esophagus. I raced up the stairs two at a time and threw open the door. I'm not sure I cared if the swinging door would hit her or not. She slipped by me and ran down the stairs. When she saw the boy, she reared back and smacked his chest with her open hand. And the look he gave her after she did it made me want to cry forever. He looked so deeply hurt. A pure hurt, as if his whole world had been shattered. He couldn't fathom why anyone would ever want to hurt him like that, let alone his own sister, whom he adored. I could see the sense of betrayal in his eyes, and there arose in me a kind of anger that everyone possesses but that no one should ever unleash. I grabbed my daughter again as my son opened wide and howled in pain.

"WHY DID YOU HIT HIM?!"

"I hate him!" she said. "He's the worst brother in the whole world and I'm going to cut his head open!"

"You apologize to him right now."

She walked up and wrapped her arms tightly around him. For half a second, it was a loving gesture. Then she laughed maniacally. When my daughter was born, I got a nice card from my uncle saying that my child's laughter would be the sweetest sound I would ever hear. But that's a lie. Children have two kinds of laughter. The first is the genuine kind, the kind my uncle was talking about. The other is the I'M-ABOUT-TO-DO-EVIL-SHIT laugh. The criminal mastermind laugh. *Mwahahahahaha.* I dread that laugh because it means someone is about to cry or something is about to fucking break. By the time a child is four or five, this is pretty much the only kind of laugh you hear out of them. The girl began squeezing her brother tighter and tighter. My son was now even more upset than when she first hit him.

"Will you let him go?" I demanded.

But she didn't. She picked him up off the floor, like a

pro wrestler about to execute a belly-to-back suplex. I pried her little fingers apart and wrested her away from him, pushing her into the stairs. At this point, the boy was a sobbing mess.

I screamed at her, "What is wrong with you? Leave him alone, god dammit!"

She smiled and hugged me and said, "I love you." She didn't mean ANY of it, which only angered me further.

"Get off of me," I told her. "You're being insincere and I can't stand it."

But she wouldn't stop hugging me. She grabbed on tight and let her entire body sag, nearly snapping my spine. Children do this all the time. They just HANG on you, like you're a monkey bar. I shook her off and she began hitting me in the stomach. She was five, so these were solid blows. She let out another horrible scream and filled the house with a thick, seemingly impenetrable kind of misery. I grabbed her and dragged her back up to her room and pinned her down on the carpet. She was laughing now. The angrier I got, the harder she laughed. I had to use every last ounce of willpower to restrain myself from kicking her ass because I very much wanted to. Inside me, there arose a voice—a voice so alien from my own that it seemed to belong to some other race of being. A terrifying, horrible voice. If my wife had heard that voice early in our relationship, she never would have married me. I grabbed the girl by the chin and blasted her with The Voice.

"WHAT IS WRONG WITH YOU?! YOU ARE

NOT RESPECTFUL! YOU WILL STAY HERE ALL NIGHT OR I SWEAR TO GOD YOU'LL BE SORRY."

I wanted her to be frightened. I wanted her to cower before The Voice. I thought about my father yelling at me when I was a kid and, oh, how I hated it. One time, I tore down a shower curtain and he yelled so loud at me that I thought my hair was gonna fall out. It scared me to death. I would have done anything as a child to not get yelled at. Even now, though I'm much older and love my father dearly, I dread it when he raises his voice. It causes me to snap right back to adolescence. I looked at my daughter and expected her to crumble, just like I did. I expected her, at long last, to give me some goddamn RESPECT. That's what all parents desperately want, and that's what drives them batshit crazy when they don't get it. Surely The Voice would get me the respect I craved.

"Faka."

And she kept on laughing. I couldn't see her anymore. I couldn't see the beautiful, intelligent, funny little girl that I knew she was. All I could see was this horrible animal. And all I could think was, *This is the moment. This is the moment when my relationship with my child turns permanently toxic.* I had always believed that you could raise your child in any number of ways and, so long as you loved them unconditionally, you could always remain on relatively good terms. Children are born good, that's what I believed. They're born good and if you love them enough, they stay that way. You hope that love is all that is required to keep your son out of jail and your daughter out of the pornography industry. But now the girl was laughing like a demon and I was terrified that things would get no better than this, that this was where the permanent rift between us would begin, the five previous years of love and—let's face it—hard work that went into raising her rendered pointless. The idea that I could love her and do my best and still get it all terribly wrong was unbearable. I was scared that the fighting would never end, that she would never calm down and just *be*, that this would be the entirety of our relationship from now on.

And I was pissed. So fucking pissed. I tried my best to lower my voice.

"Please," I told her, "I'm very close to hurting you right now. Please don't make me hurt you. Why don't we, I dunno, talk about dinner? What would you like for dinner?"

"Candy."

"Not candy."

"Candy!"

The Voice returned. "GOD DAMMIT, NOT CANDY!" I smacked the floor hard enough to break my hand. Still no fear in her eyes.

"Faka."

"Fine," I said. "You want me to spank you? Here we go."

I jerked her up and sat down on one of the little kiddie chairs in her bedroom. I laid her across my lap as she alternated between laughing and shrieking. This was my first time performing an attempted spanking. I looked at her backside and tried to figure out a course of action. *Do you pull the pants down? You don't pull the pants down, right? That would just be weird. How hard are you supposed to spank? Is it supposed to really hurt? It's gotta hurt, right? If it doesn't hurt, then they don't get the message.* I gave a gentle test blow and nothing happened. Then I spanked a little bit harder and she kept on laughing.

I felt like a fucking idiot. I don't even know how spanking became the go-to method of corporal punishment. It's bizarre. All I could think about while spanking her was that it wasn't working, and that the only thing spanking does is set your child up for a life of sexual deviancy. The creepiness of the whole enterprise is right there, out in the open. I took my daughter off my lap and tried to play nice.

"Please, I don't wanna fight like this."

She laughed in my face, practically spitting into it. "Faka."

Again with that fucking word. I wished that she knew the real swearword so that we could simply get it over with. The anger bubbled up again and I could feel two shades of it. I was angry at my daughter for acting up, obviously. But the far greater anger came from my own self-loathing. I was failing as a parent. Miserably. And even though I was failing in private, it didn't feel that way. I felt as if the whole world was watching me fuck up. That was the real source of anger—that feeling of incompetence, of such obvious, visible powerlessness.

When I was single and saw parents losing it with their kids, I used to frown at them. *I'll never be like that,* I promised myself. But single people are pathetically naive. They don't know what it's like to spend fourteen consecutive hours with a child. They don't understand how that massive span of time allows for every single possible human emotion to be bared: anger, fear, jealousy, love . . . all of it. More to the point, they don't realize what little assholes kids can be. They have no idea. When I was in middle school, they brought in a lady who had traveled to the South Pole to speak to us. She told us that, at one point during the trip, she became so cold and so desperate for food that she ate an entire stick of butter. We all were disgusted. But she was like, "Yeah, well, if you had been at the South Pole, you would have had butter for dinner too." Parenting is similar in that you end up acting in ways that your younger self would have found repellent because the circumstances overwhelm you. What I'm basically saying is that having kids is like being stuck in Antarctica.

I'm not sure any group of parents has ever been subjected to as much widespread derision as the current generation of American parents. We are told, constantly, how badly we are fucking our kids up. There are scores of books being sold every day that demonstrate how much better parents are in China, and in France, and in the Amazon River Basin. I keep waiting for a *New York Times* article about how leaders of the Cali drug cartel excel at teaching their children self-reliance.

And it's not just books shitting on us. We hear it from our own parents, who go to pathological lengths to remind us that we hover too much, or that we let the kids watch too much TV, or that we're letting our kids eat too much processed dogshit. We're SOFT. That's the stereotype. We're soft parents, and our kids will grow up to be free-range terrorists because of it. We see the stereotype in movies and ads and TV shows and on the news, in study after study that says our kids are getting dumber and fatter and angrier. We've ruined everything. Collectively, all this empirical evidence of our shittiness is destroying our confidence, our ability to handle our kids with any measure of assuredness.

The funny thing is that I think the evidence is probably wrong. Fifty years ago, spanking and other forms of corporal punishment were far more widespread. Fathers were distant and uncommunicative. Everyone smoked in front of their kids. Seat belts were for pussies. And if parents had any kind of problem with their child, they didn't have the Internet on hand to help find a solution, or at least a sympathetic ear. We have that now, and it makes us better. No parents I know suffer a kid's shitty eating habits for long. They're willing to look for help right away, and they can find it, and that matters. That counts for something. We're not *that* bad, I swear. But the stereotype shrouds all of that.

We even hear the stereotype from fellow parents. We're constantly judging and grading other parents, just to make sure that they aren't any better than us. I'm as guilty as anyone. I see some lady hand her kid a Nintendo DS at the supermarket and I instantly downgrade that lady to Shitty Parent status. I feel pressure to live up to a parental ideal that no one probably has ever achieved. I feel pressure to raise a group of human beings that will help America kick the shit out of Finland and South Korea in the world math rankings. I feel pressure to shield my kids from the trillion pages of hentai donkey porn out there on the Internet. I feel pressure to make the insane amounts of money needed for a suppos-edly "middle-class" upbringing for the kids, an upbringing that includes a house and college tuition and health care and so many other expenses that you have to be a multimillion-aire to afford it. PRESSURE PRESSURE PRESSURE.

And the worst part is that none of those external forces can begin to match the pressure I bring to bear on myself. The fact that I had resorted to grabbing and spanking and willfully inflicting harm on my own child made me feel like a criminal. I felt like, if someone had videotaped the whole episode, I would have been thrown in jail forever. Maybe I deserved to be there. Maybe everyone else was good at keep-ing their shit together and I wasn't. I alone was the Worst Dad on Earth—the kind of dad that gets entire memoirs written about him by his kids, about living with him and his horrible demons. Maybe I was an abuser. Even telling you this story now, I feel like I'm edging off the details because I'm terrified of admitting how hard I grabbed my daughter's arm. As a matter of fact, I smacked her once. I can't tell you where or why because it makes me feel ugly and I don't want you reading it and demanding that my kids be taken from me. I don't remember my dad ever smacking me. He may have yelled a few times, but nothing that dramatic. Why was I so much worse of a parent? Why didn't my kid respect and fear me the way I respected and feared my old man? Why did my children always require one more minute of patience than I had? And why was I losing my shit at a five-year-old for acting like a five-year-old?

The girl was still screaming and driving me to the

precipice of madness, and I searched around in my mind for some kind of creative solution. I definitely wanted to punish her. I couldn't even recall what we were fighting about, which happens a lot when you fight with a child. The fight becomes its own reason for being. I wanted to prove my dominance over the household, to regain control. I wanted to WIN, which is foolish because there's no prize for defeating a fucking five-year-old at something.

Then I thought, *a shower*. A cold shower. That's humane, right? It doesn't hurt the child. It just offers a dose of surprise refreshment. The more I mulled it over, the more I was convinced it was a good idea, which is NOT TRUE.

"Listen to me," I said to the girl. "I need you to calm down and I need you to promise me you'll never hit your brother again. Or else, you're getting a cold shower." Secretly, I think I wanted her to make me do it. Seemed like a worthy experiment.

"Faka."

"All right, then."

I grabbed her and brought her to the bathroom and undressed her. I turned on the shower as she tried to slip out of my grasp.

"No, Daddy! NONONONONO!" she said.

"You will have to learn."

I put her in and when the cold water smashed against her body, the tone of her screaming changed from anger to sadness. I could hear the shift. I could feel it splitting me open, leaking all the poisonous anger out of me. Her skin went taut with cold and she tried desperately to get away from the water, as if it were attacking her. *The fuck am I doing?* I pulled her out and she clung to me, crying her eyes out. She was heartbroken.

"Sweetheart, I just wanted you to listen."

And she looked me dead in the eye and shouted out, "BUT I LOVE YOU!"

That was all she needed to say to leave me utterly defeated. She loved me and I had just done something that made it seem like I didn't love her back. The regret was instant and total. I loved her. I loved her more than anything in the world and I didn't even know how we got to this point and now that we were here I felt so dumb, so unbelievably fucking dumb. I took a towel and I wrapped it around her and I wept on her shoulder as I dried her off. "I'm sorry," I said to her. "I'm so sorry. I love you too. I just . . . I hate fighting. I don't wanna fight with you. Am I a bad father? I feel like I'm doing a horrible job."

I wanted her to say, "No." I wanted one of those little movie moments where the child turns all precocious and offers words of wisdom to a failing parent. But the girl just ignored me instead. I dried her off and sent her back to her room to get dressed, which she did quietly. I came back downstairs and lay facedown on the floor, crying and pounding the carpet in frustration. My son came out of the playroom and walked up to me, like a dog walking up to sniff a dead body.

"Deddy, are woo oat-kay?"

"I'm okay. Thank you. Thank you so much for asking. I love you guys. I just wish I knew how to figure this out."

He ran away and I scraped myself off the floor. Every time I have a fight with my kids, I feel like I have to start from scratch. I feel like I've tumbled back down the mountain, as if all the good effort I've put in before has gone to waste and I've fucked everything up permanently. All I want are streaks—little runs of good parenting days. I have a vision in my head of a never-ending streak—a time when I have a perfect relationship with my children that involves mutual respect and lots of outward affection. I don't know if that's a real thing or just some pipe dream that only adds to the pressure. Getting up off the floor, I felt like that mythical tipping point was even further away from me now. All I wanted was to get there, and I wasn't gonna give up. It's so easy to turn your child into a villain and let yourself hate your life, but you can't. You can't let misery win out because it will destroy everything.

I composed myself and swore I would never again throw gas on the fire to escalate the conflict. All I had to do was walk away from the girl and the fight would have been over before all this horrible shit happened, but I didn't. My wife came through the door and I shuddered to tell her everything that had happened: The Voice, the arm grab, the spanking, the shower. I didn't want her to know any of it. But I have a big mouth. Nothing stays inside this vault for very long.

"Everything okay?" she asked.

"She hit him and I lost my shit," I said.

"It's all right."

"I spanked her. I'm so fucking sorry. I spanked her and

I tried giving her a cold shower to get her to stop being horrible and it was all so stupid."

"It's all right. It's all right. I've spanked her too."

"You have?"

"Oh, yeah," she said. "It does nothing."

"Why doesn't it do anything? I want it to WORK."

"I know! I wish it would."

"Why don't they listen to us? What's wrong with them? I did whatever my dad told me to. In fact, I did what he told me to do just now. And I'm *thirty-five*, for shit's sake."

"I dunno. Just don't spank her again. It makes everything worse."

"I made it so much worse, you have no idea."

"It's all right."

My daughter came down the stairs and there was no more screaming or evil laughter. She had been replaced with an actual girl, the one I'd kill for. She didn't seem to have any hard feelings about our power struggle. Kids affect a kind of multiple personality disorder—they become entirely different people for a bit and then have no recollection of that identity once the storm has passed.

"Can I get you something to eat?" I asked her.

"Shells and cheese," she said.

At last, a sincere answer. That was all I ever wanted. Plain, mature sincerity. I hugged her and told her I loved her and she pushed me away with a laugh. A nice laugh.

"Dad, ew."

She went to go draw a picture and I began climbing the mountain all over again, hoping to string together enough good days of parenting until I got to the point where there were no more bad days, until the day when I could stand proud in front of stern newscasters and judgmental foreigners and overbearing grandparents and anyone else who thought I sucked at this and tell them that I was a good father and have them believe it.

HODDUB

My parents had come down to visit us and were staying in a nearby hotel. The kids went absolutely batshit insane when my folks were in town because they got to visit the hotel, ride in the glass elevator, order room service (thirty dollars for a burger), and play in the indoor pool. My son, now three years old, thought my parents lived in this hotel, and every time we drove by it he demanded to see them.

"Dat Gammy and Papa's hodel."

"Actually, they live in Connecticut," I said. "They only stay at that hotel when they visit us. Otherwise another person stays in their room."

That pissed him off. "DAT GAMMY AND PAPA'S WOMB!"

"It's not their room."

"It ID they womb!"

Now my parents were finally in town and staying at the precious hotel, and I brought the two kids by because, as always, we needed something to do. I brought everything they needed for the indoor pool: suits, goggles, floaty vests, après-swim sarongs, the whole deal.

It was nine in the morning and the pool had just opened. There was a lifeguard there who couldn't have been more than seventeen years old. The pool had a hot tub attached to it, with a tile partition separating the hot tub from the main pool. You could leap over the partition into the big pool with relative ease.

My kids both wanted to start off in the hot tub, but there was a sign on the wall that said children under five weren't permitted in the hot tub. I assume the thinking was that if a very small child got into the hot tub, a witch would burst through the door, add chopped carrots and onions to the water, and attempt to make a stew out of your little one. So my son wasn't supposed to go in. But we had been to this pool before and the lifeguard the last time didn't seem to give a shit. Some teenage lifeguards let you flagrantly disobey pool policy because they're teenage lifeguards and they have more important things to do, like stare at their own abs. But others can be shockingly aggressive in enforcing every rule on the list, and the lifeguard on duty this day fell into this category. My son took one step down into the hot tub and he blew his whistle, which hardly seemed necessary because we were two feet away from him.

"He can't go in there," he said.

"Really?" I asked. That was the best counterargument I could muster.

"Yeah, no, he's not allowed in there."

So I had to calmly explain to my son that he wasn't allowed in the hot tub. But you can't just say NO to a kid. That pisses them off. You have to spin it. You have to make it sound like the fact that they've been barred from the hot tub is some kind of awesome development.

"Hey, you know what?" I said to him. "The lifeguard said you can go in the big kid pool!"

My son didn't take the bait. He knew I was bullshitting him. "I WAND TO BO IN DA HODDUB."

Meanwhile, my daughter wasn't helping things because she was frolicking in the tub and rubbing his face in it. "I can go in the hot tub!" she yelled. "See? It's easy! You just jump right in! Come on, jump!"

"He can't do that," I said. "Why don't you help me out and go in the big kid pool?"

"That pool is cold."

Another family came into the pool area while my son was crying, which was embarrassing because you want to keep the moments when your kids lose their shit private and not have everyone around come check it out. There was a girl who was roughly my daughter's age, and when she jumped into the big pool, my daughter nearly broke her ankles following suit. Now she was in the big pool, swimming around with her head just above the water, like a Labrador in the ocean, and I thought I had it made. I could have kissed that other little girl, if kissing a little girl that is not your own didn't result in a jail sentence.

I turned to my son and pointed at his sister. "See? She's in the big pool now. Let's go!"

He stood his ground. When my son says no, it's like he's winding up to throw a baseball at your head. "NnnnnnnnnnnnnO!"

He walked over to the hot tub and sat down on the first step. By then, I was so eager to end the standoff that I turned to the lifeguard and was like, "That's okay, right?" After all, it was just one step. Witches don't come flying in until full submersion, right? The lifeguard was down with it. I breathed easy.

Then the boy took another step down. Now he was up to his knees in the water. I turned to the lifeguard for approval and he shook his head. One step was okay. Two steps? PRISON. I gently told my son that he had to scoot back up one step.

"NnnnnnnnnnnnnO!"

"Just go up one step and we'll be okay."

"Nnnnnnn—"

"Don't say it."

"—nnnnnO!"

"Why don't we forget the hot tub and get pancakes?"

"No. I wand hoddub."

Somehow I always ended up in these kind of situations when parenting. *Don't take two steps into the hot tub. Please only eat half that banana. You can watch TV for twelve more minutes but not thirteen.* Children are like very small terrorists: You cannot negotiate with them.

My son got up and began making quick little steps up and down. That was his "I have to pee" dance, and it never ceased to put me into panic mode. I became terrified that piss would come exploding out of all of his orifices if I didn't get him to a nearby toilet. So I looked at him and asked him, out loud . . .

"Oh, do you have to pee?"

Never say this to a child out loud at a public pool. Ever. You have to be a fucking moron to announce to everyone that your child is about to urinate in the pool, and I apparently was dumb enough to qualify. Everyone heard me. The lifeguard heard me. The other family heard me. For all I know, the lifeguard was already contacting the police.

Then my mom chimed in, "Oh, you need to get him out of the hot tub, Drew."

"I know, Mom."

"He can't just pee in there."

"I KNOW!"

I begged my son to get out of the hot tub and he stood his ground. I considered picking him up and bringing him to the bathroom by force, but my son did not take kindly to forced bathroom trips. If you picked him up when he didn't want to be picked up, he became possessed by Satan and began thrashing about while speaking in ancient Aramaic. So with everyone at the pool staring daggers at me, I begged the boy to exit the hot tub.

"Please, man. You need to get out and go potty."

"NnnnnnnnnnnnnnO!"

"I'll give you a thousand dollars."

But it was too late. My son stopped his little quick steps, and I could see the yellow legs of urine streaming down his inner thigh. Everyone watching knew what had happened, so I had no choice. I picked up my son mid-piss and he predictably began trying to claw my face off. I wasn't gonna be able to carry the demon child all the way to the pisser, so I set him down in a far corner of the pool area, on the tile floor, and let him finish there. As if no one would know what I was doing.

"You can't just let him pee on the floor."

"Shut up, Mom."

Everyone was still staring while my son made a little puddle around himself. There was a stack of complimentary towels nearby and I grabbed three of them to soak up the piss, which surely violated hotel pool towel etiquette. Those things were not meant to be piss sponges. All the while, I avoided the lifeguard's gaze.

The other family got out of the pool and fled, and that pissed me off. *Those hypocrites*, I thought. When you go into a public pool, you tacitly agree to the fact that you will be bathing in ten thousand gallons of chlorinated urine. I wouldn't have sold out another parent like that. But this family left, trying to paint my boy as a common pool-pissing thug, which was bullshit.

I finished cleaning up the piss and my son demanded to go back in the hot tub. I didn't want to stay there a second longer. We had already been branded with the scarlet P. I didn't want to bring my son back into the hot tub with that lifeguard still there. But the boy was stubborn, and I was a sap, so back into the tub he went.

It was unbearable. I could feel the lifeguard's eyes on me. I wanted to get away from all this as fast as possible and settle down with a Dutch Baby at the Original Pancake House. I didn't want to be trapped in this Victorian pissing drama a second longer. I grabbed my son.

"We have to leave."

"NnnnnnnnnnnnnnO!"

"I'll let you push every button on the elevator."

"Oat-kay!"

Out of the pool he sprung. I quickly toweled him off, grabbed my daughter, and headed for the exit with my folks, who said nothing. On the way, I put on my best face and said to the lifeguard, "Thank you!"

He said nothing back.

Then my son said, "Deddy, I peed in da hoddub!"

And I nudged him out the door.

THE CREEK AND
THE COFFEE CUP

I was attempting to go out for a power walk. I couldn't do any running or sprinting because I had a bad back, but if I listened to enough speed metal while power walking, I could convince myself that I was actually running and that I looked crazy athletic while doing it. The reality was that I looked like an eighty-year-old person doing laps at 6:00 A.M. around an empty shopping mall to help prevent leg clots. Sometimes I even walked in place in front of the TV. I hope no one ever videotaped me doing this.

My wife was in the office on the computer. The kids were finished with lunch and now watching TV. They hadn't started getting bored and kicking each other in the face just yet. There was an opening for me to go work out—a bare sliver of time for me to get my shit together and squeeze out the door without any loud objections. When you're a single person, working out is a horrible thing. The idea of hauling your ass to a gym to labor on a treadmill for forty-five minutes is terrifying when you could be out drinking or trying to hook up with a blond paralegal. But when you're married and have children, working out is ECSTASY. Running (or power walking) five miles is nothing when you have no children or grocery bags weighing you down. It's like spending a week at Canyon Ranch. The kids themselves are inherently wonderful and lovely and made of honey rainbows and all that nonsense. But the work involved in feeding them and clothing them and making sure they don't finger-bang the wall socket is what's so draining.

Also, children make you very fat. I always hoped that the time I spent every day installing car seats and carrying unruly little fuckers up to the bath would help burn off all the calories I consumed, but that was never the case. There were too many birthday party sheet cakes, too many bowls of uneaten Kraft Mac that I despised throwing away and had to eat myself, too many pieces of Halloween candy. I couldn't resist any of it, so parenting had become a six-year stint grazing at a corporate off-site buffet: an endless stretch of mindless eating. I hated myself when I ate that much birthday cake, but it wasn't my fault that Safeway sprinkled crystal meth into every corner piece. So, so good.

Taking a power walk would probably burn off a whopping thirty calories, but at least it would make me feel like I was attempting to stem the tide. I got my shirt and shorts and socks and an iPod mini that I kept housed in an unwashed armband, a vile piece of nylon with sweat stains that were old enough to be carbon-dated—a garment that smelled so bad, it could wake smoke inhalation victims. This garment kept people away from me, which suited me just fine. Working out was my time to bask in the sanctuary of aloneness.

But my daughter saw me in my workout clothes and immediately jumped off the couch in alarm. Kids can tell when you're about to ditch them.

"Where are you going?" she asked.

"I'm going for a walk."

"Can I come?"

"This is a serious walk. I walk real fast. HARDCORE."

"I can walk fast."

"We're gonna walk far. Like, five miles."

"So what? Who cares? It's easy."

"You've never walked five miles before."

"Sure I have. It's EASY."

Everything was easy to the girl. She was six now and eager to let everyone know that she could accomplish any task, even one she had never previously attempted, with minimal effort. Cartwheels? EASY. Jumping off a swing from eight feet in the air? EASY. Cold fusion? EASY-PEASY LEMON SQUEEZY. She had an impenetrable reality distortion field.

"You sure you don't wanna watch TV or something?" I asked her.

"I wanna go with you."

"All right. You can come. But just know that I don't stop. You gotta keep up. And I'm gonna listen to awesome music the whole time. NO TALKIN' WHILE I'M A-ROCKIN'."

"It's easy."

She put on her sneakers and grabbed the little clip-on radio my wife had bought for her at Target. It was programmed to the only station she liked and it allowed her to listen to all the Flo Rida she wanted without me ever, ever having to hear it. She was not allowed to have an iPod, even though she was now old enough to be hired by one of Apple's Chinese subcontractors to make one herself. I strapped on my noxious armband and we walked outside together. I got into full power-walking-dipshit mode: ass tight, chest out, arms a-pumpin'. I built up a head of steam and now I was in full "pretend Olympic sprinter" mode.

My daughter remained ten yards behind me, pausing every so often because her earbuds would fall out and she had to put them back in. It's as if they designed earbuds specifically so that they fall out of your ears every third step. Eventually, she caught up to me.

"Can you not go so fast?" she asked.

I was pleased that she thought I was fast. I felt like I was leaving a trail of fire in my wake. "This is what I told you," I said. "I go fast. You gotta keep up. Let's go."

"Okay."

We got onto a park trail and walked at a brisk pace through the woods alongside a large creek. Every thirty seconds, I would turn my head to make sure the girl was still behind me, and that no one had grabbed her and forced her into slave labor. But she never fell too far behind. She kept chugging along, taking strides that were half the length of mine but somehow walking fast enough to not lose any ground. I began to warm to the idea of having her there. I thought, *This is the beginning. We'll do this every day and one day she'll become an Olympic race walker even though she was gifted with no athletic genes of any sort. Power moseying will become the girl's passion. She'll never want to watch TV or play a video game again. She's just gonna be all about the moseying. And we'll forge an unbreakable bond and never fight again. We might join forces and become a pair of power walking spies, chasing down rogue agents with our relentless four-mile-per-hour pacing.*

As we walked, a sweaty old guy merged with us from one of the path's many tributaries and walked at the exact same pace as us, which aggravated me to no end. The girl and I were enjoying a special power walking moment. Did this man know nothing of basic power walking etiquette? I deliberately sped up the pace to leave the geezer behind, and the girl kept up. I assumed that we had lost him for good.

We passed by campgrounds and playgrounds and kids throwing rocks into the creek and she didn't get distracted like a little puppy. She was focused and alert and kicking much ass. I saw her tiring down but that only made me want to walk faster, just to test her stamina level. Near the creek, the girl spotted an empty coffee mug sitting on a concrete ledge. She ran up to me and tugged at my shirt. I took out one earphone.

"There was a coffee cup there!" she said.

"Yeah, that was weird."

"Who do you think it belongs to?"

"I dunno," I said.

"Well, it sure is weird."

"Yeah, it is. I like walking with you."

"I like walking with you too. Umm, Dad?"

"Yeah."

"Do you think you could stop listening to your music?"

"Sure."

I took out my headphones and put them in my pocket and we continued on, across big roads and past houses and churches and strange new intersections that the girl had never seen before, that *I* had never seen before. It was farther from home than I ever went on my own. I reveled in the joy of happening upon all these new lands as we walked. It was like we were progressing to the next level of a video game with every mile. *There's a broadsword behind that tree!* Somehow we ended up walking much farther than I ever thought we would together. I thought we'd go five hundred feet and then the girl would ask to go home and have brownies. But on and on we went, and I was so happy to explore new terrain with the girl that I never made the sensible move of turning us around before she was too tired to make it back.

"We gotta turn around," I finally told her. "Can you make it home? Because I don't have a phone and we can't get Mom to pick us up."

"I can make it."

We turned around and started back home. By the time we were halfway back, my daughter was working up a sweat and visibly laboring with each step. And while I was proud of myself for pushing her to walk farther than she ever had, I now felt like an insane sports parent that deprives his kid of water and ends up watching her die of heatstroke. I stopped her.

"Let's rest for a second," I said.

"Okay."

We were still on the path, with a wide swath of grass to one side and the creek to the other. We stopped by the concrete ledge we had seen earlier, and the coffee cup was still resting on top of it.

"That coffee cup is still there," I said.

"Why's it still there?" the girl asked. "It's weird. That cup is a stupid cup."

I walked up to the cup and grabbed it. It was empty and had old ring stains on the bottom. Whoever left it there wasn't coming back for it. Beyond the ledge was an outcropping of rocks that gradually submerged down into the creek. I took the cup back to my daughter as she rested on the open park lawn.

"What should we do with it?" I asked.

"I dunno."

And for reasons still unknown to me, I was gripped with the sudden urge to smash the thing on the rocks below. I had all kinds of rationalizations for doing it pop up in my brain. *The girl's come so far and I don't have any treat to give her or water to drink. She deserves to do something cool. It would bring us even closer together. And the mug is made of clay. Clay is natural! If we smash it on the rocks, it will* become *the rocks! We'll be sending it back into nature. SMASHING SHIT IS FUN.*

"Come with me," I said to her.

"What are we doing?"

"It's a surprise. You see anyone else around?"

She looked up and down the path. "No one's coming."

"Good. Here, take this coffee cup and smash it on the rocks."

"Really?"

"Yeah. Really."

"But that's littering. That's bad for the earth."

"It's not littering. It's . . . free-range recycling. Give it a shot. It'll be cool."

"Okay."

She took the cup and flung it down onto the rocks, where it smashed into a thousand pieces. Oh, what a fantastic sound it made. I felt like I had just hit a baseball five hundred feet. I desperately wished there were another two dozen coffee cups stacked around us so that we could smash them over and over again. There's something immensely satisfying about destroying things. Children know this all too well. Eventually, you grow old and you learn to not break things. But you never lose the sense of elation that comes from breaking them. That lies dormant inside you until the day you decide to take your kid out for some petty vandalism.

I was marveling at the shattered pottery scattered about the rocks when I heard footsteps behind us. I turned and saw the same old guy who had kept pace with us earlier run by. He had seen us throwing the coffee cup. He was staring at us and I looked away because I hated having his eyes on me. I grabbed the girl.

"We gotta go."

"That was so cool!" she said.

"I know, but now we gotta get out of here."

We started walking back home, with the old guy forty

yards in front of us. I made certain to keep our distance so that we wouldn't catch up and come face-to-face with him. But then all of us came to an intersection and the DON'T WALK sign was up and blinking. The old man stopped, and now we were in danger of catching up to him before the light turned. I slowed down to a crawl, as if I were walking in place. I thought about stopping forty yards from the light and milling around, but that would have felt even more conspicuous. So my daughter and I strolled to the light and I steadfastly avoided eye contact.

"You know, I saw you throw that cup," the old man said to me.

Guhhhhhhhhh.

I turned to him. "Oh?"

"I'm on the Rock Creek Preservation Committee."

Are you fucking shitting me? "Oh."

"Yeah, we're trying to keep garbage out of the creek, not put more garbage into it."

"I'm sorry. I'm really sorry. It won't happen again."

"That's just my opinion on the matter."

"I get it. I totally see where you're coming from. I'm sorry." The light still hadn't changed and now I wanted to leap in front of an oncoming Metrobus.

We stood there for ten more painful seconds until the WALK sign flashed and we could finally cross. The girl and I scampered over to the other side and turned left to go home. The old man kept on going straight, and I whispered a little thank-you to the heavens when he finally vanished out of sight. I pictured him going home and calling the police on me. It was imperative that my daughter and I get home as quickly as possible and hide in the basement so that law enforcement officials could never track us down.

"What did that man say?" the girl asked me.

"He said we shouldn't litter."

"Did we litter?"

"We, uh . . . Look, we're not gonna do it again. That was just a one-time deal. Don't go throwing stuff into rivers or else people will get mad. You understand?"

"Mmm-hmm."

The next day, I put on all my workout clothes and the gross iPod armband. My daughter was splayed out on the couch watching TV, each of her limbs resting on a different cushion. I walked up to her.

"I'm going for another walk," I said. "You wanna come?"

"Nah," she said.

"Really? But we had a great time last time."

"Nah. I don't wanna."

"I won't listen to music."

"Nah."

"We don't have to walk as fast. Or as far."

"Nah."

"We could smash another coffee cup."

"Dad! You can't litter!"

"No, I suppose we can't."

Sometimes you can't get a kid out of the house until you walk out the door. So I put on my socks and my sneakers and made it clear to the girl that I was prepared to leave without her.

"I'm putting on my socks."

No reply.

"I'm putting on my sneakers now."

No reply.

"I am now opening the door."

No reply.

"I am now opening the screen door, which is the last barrier between myself and the outside."

No reply.

The door slammed shut behind me and I found myself out for a walk, alone. I set out down the path toward the creek where the girl had walked for over an hour and engaged with me in petty misdemeanors. I was unencumbered, free to power walk as fast or as slow as I pleased. It didn't feel anywhere near as liberating as it used to.

ELECTRIC TOOTHBRUSH

I bought my son an electric toothbrush because trying to brush his teeth manually had become a nightly exercise in forcible mouth sodomy. Kids don't understand why they have to put toothpaste on a brush and scrub their teeth for twenty agonizing seconds, and even if you tell them why—*Your teeth will fall out! Girls will never kiss you!*—they still don't get it.

I tried bribing my son. I tried reverse psychology by saying, "Whoa, hey, don't go brushing those teeth! That would get you in big trouble, amigo." I tried doing that thing they suggest in parenting books where you say to your kid, "Your teeth aren't brushed!" This presents them with a problem to solve. *My teeth are not brushed; therefore, I must brush them.* The idea is that most children like solving problems rather than being told what to do. You can't ask them to brush their teeth because that gives them a chance to say no. The phrasing must be precise, like the wording of a will.

But the boy was no sap. He knew that he was three years old and had NO problems of any sort. No life-form on earth has it easier than a three-year-old child. You don't have to go to school, you don't have to have a job, and you're perfectly happy having a train for a best friend. What did he need to solve a problem for? Problems were for bigger, dumber people. He could have given a shit about his unbrushed teeth.

So every night, I had to grab his big head and jam the brush into his mouthhole and he cried and screamed and acted as if I were a Hanoi prison guard toying with his psyche. Fed up with this process, I bought an electric toothbrush and put all kinds of cool stickers on it, hoping he might come to enjoy brushing his teeth.

"Look, it's got a motor!" I said. "It's a toy! You can blast all the bad plaque goblins with it!" You have to make everything sound fun to a child. Brushing your teeth is *blasting plaque goblins*. Broccoli soup is *monster* soup. A trip to the drugstore is a trip to the *witch's laboratory*. It gets tiring.

I put some toothpaste on the new toothbrush (we bought five different kinds of paste before finding one that suited his palate), turned it on, and handed it to him. He ran into my room with it, threw it on the ground so that the toothpaste could pick up random hairs and bits of lint, then pulled down his underwear and started grabbing his dick. I rinsed the brush off, put on more paste, and handed it back to him.

"Once you brush your teeth, Daddy will tell you a story."

Slowly but surely, my son turned the brush on, raised

the brush to his mouth, and placed it on one of his teeth. Massive success. I felt as if I'd just deadlifted five hundred pounds. Only fifteen some-odd teeth to go and my effort would be an official triumph. I figured that now the brush was in his mouth, we'd be cruising.

Instead, the boy took the brush out of his mouth and stared down at his dick. Then he looked up at me. I knew what was coming next. There are those moments when you know exactly what's going to happen, only you're powerless to stop it.

I screamed out, "NOT ON YOUR PENIS, NOOOOO!!!"

But he was too fast and I was too old and fat. The vibrating brush went right down onto his dick, which I'm sure felt terrific to him. And then, once the boy felt his dick was sufficiently brushed, he stuck it back in his mouth. Then he giggled.

My mom was visiting, because of course she was. Weird shit like this only happens when grandparents visit, as if the children wait for that exact moment to make you look bad. I went down and told her what happened, and I assumed she and I would have a good laugh over it. *He brushed his peener, HA HA! Kids brush the damnedest things!*

Instead, she quickly inhaled through clenched teeth, the way you do when you watch someone tell a bad joke during a wedding toast.

"Oh, Drew."

She looked truly concerned, as if I were raising a goddamn criminal. It wasn't my fault, Mom. I didn't tell him to brush his dick and then eat it. And don't think you would have done any better.

Ever since that night, I have instituted the following rule in our house: *No one is allowed to brush his or her teeth without pants on. Ever.* It was one of those commonsense rules I never would have thought of ten years ago because I was single and alone and had yet to meet anyone who enjoyed brushing his own penis.

NITS

My daughter had just gotten home from school and my wife pulled me aside to speak to me in hushed tones.

"Did you hear about Marshall Reilly?" she asked me.

"Who is that? Is that a famous person?"

"It's one of her classmates."

"Oh. Really?"

"Yes, really. You've met his mother several times."

"I have?"

"You know! She has brown hair. Her husband's name is Mike. He's a lawyer."

"(blank stare)"

"Anyway, the point is that he's in her class, and he got head lice this week. We got a note about it."

"HEAD LICE?!"

"Shhhhh!"

"Oh man, that's gross as shit," I said.

"Isn't it?"

"Do they not bathe him? Does the kid play in the toilet all day?"

"I don't know, but we should keep an eye on her."

"Pfft. She's not gonna get head lice. She takes a bath every day. She's a pretty little girl. Only fat boys who smell like old clams get head lice."

"I'm sure she won't, but I don't like the idea of the head lice kid going to school with her every day."

"She'll be fine," I said. "No way she gets head lice."

Many Months Later

The girl got off the school bus on a Friday afternoon scratching her head and I thought nothing of it. She scratched it as she walked down the street. She scratched it while she was watching TV. She scratched it while she ate dinner, and while she colored in her coloring book, and while she begged me for an ice cream sandwich. At some point, after hours and hours of scratching, enough to tear off her own scalp, I finally connected the dots.

"Hey," I said to my wife, "she sure is scratching her head a lot."

My wife's eyes widened. "I was just gonna say that!"

"Maybe she has dandruff. I have lots of dandruff. Look . . ." I scratched my head and thirty pounds of dead skin sloughed off. "Dandruff."

"I'm worried she has lice."

"No way."

"Remember when Marshall Reilly got it?"

"Who?"

"One of her classmates. You've met his mother several times."

"I have?"

"You know! She has brown hair. Her husband's name is Mike. He's a lawyer."

"(blank stare)"

"Oh, for God's sake. I'm gonna check her."

"Don't do that. She's fine."

I was trying to keep my wife away from the girl's hair because little girls do not like it when you touch their hair. Every time I dared to approach my daughter with a hairbrush, she would scream as if she were being subjected to Civil War–era surgery. Then I would tell her to stop screaming and she would scream even *louder*, and then I would brush her hair anyway as punishment for all that screaming. This was not a healthy way of doing things. My daughter will probably grow up with an intense fear of hair. Wigs will scare her to death. She'll marry a guy with alopecia and that will be that.

So I was averse to exploring the girl's scalp, but my wife was more than happy to attack other people's heads. At random hours, she would walk up to me and begin looking through my hair without even bothering to ask me if that was something I wanted. If I had an eye booger, she would jam a finger into my eye socket without so much as a warning. And she happily assaulted the girl with a hairbrush for minutes at a time every morning. She had no fear of reprisals. She'd be great at mugging people.

She walked up to our daughter, who was parked in front of the TV, and began rooting through her hair.

"What are you doing?" the girl yelled. "STOP!"

"I'm checking your hair," my wife said.

"Go away!" she said, burying her head in one of the throw cushions on the couch.

"No, no, no! Don't put your head there. If you have lice, they'll get in the cushion."

"STOP!"

"Drew, I see little things in here. Come look."

I stared down into my daughter's wriggling head and saw a bunch of little blond capsules, as wide as two hairs across. They were shiny, almost greasy in appearance.

"It's probably dandruff," I said.

"That's not dandruff."

Now the research began. My wife hopped onto the computer, Googled "head lice symptoms," and opened up every single link.

"Look here," she said. "It says, 'Nits resemble tiny pussy willow buds. Nits can be mistaken for dandruff, but unlike dandruff, they can't be easily brushed out of hair.' That's what she has."

"You're overreacting," I said. At this point, I was like the clueless sheriff you see in movies, the last guy to acknowledge that aliens have invaded.

"Well, let's look at the pictures and see," she said. I tried to stop her from clicking "IMAGES" because when you search for an illness on Google Image Search, it gives you photos of the ugliest people imaginable exhibiting the worst symptoms imaginable. Also, you get a picture of a penis, for no reason at all.

But I was too late. She hit search and I was confronted with a mosaic of severely lice-ridden scalps. Nits, nits everywhere. Bleeding heads. Broken skin. Pus-filled abscesses. In the center of it all was a photo of an adult louse, swollen to ten times its size after feasting on a child's blood. Oh God, it was so awful. I can still see it in my head even though I don't want to.

"Close the browser! Close the browser!" I said.

"You see now? She has it."

"It could still be dandruff."

"Oh my God, Drew. What is wrong with you? Can you please accept reality here?"

I still clung to the now-infinitesimal chance of this all being an elaborate ruse. I didn't want it to be head lice because I didn't want to deal with what was certain to be a world of bullshit involved in ridding my daughter of it. I stood in the dining room and watched from afar as my wife went back and dug into my daughter's head.

"STOP!!!!"

"Honey, hold still," my wife told her. "You definitely have lice."

"I do?"

I ran to my wife and tried to correct her. "Shhh! Don't say she has lice in front of her! She'll get embarrassed!"

"I really have lice?" my daughter asked.

"You *might* have lice," I said. "It's not definitive. No need to think of yourself as filthy or diseased just yet."

"There are nits all over her hair," my wife said. Then she struck gold. "Oh my God. There it is." She reached into the girl's hair and plucked off a tiny little black speck with legs, then held it up like it was a fugitive that she had been hunting down for years. "This is one of them," she said triumphantly.

I stared at it. To the naked eye, a head louse doesn't look all *that* bad. It's just a little tiny thing. It's when you hop on the Internet and look at one that's been magnified fifty times over that the sheer horror of it hits you.

"What if it's a flea?" I asked.

"You're gonna have to go to CVS and pick up some shampoo."

"Really?"

"Yes, really. I'm gonna call the doctor. We have to strip all the beds in the house. We have to wash all her clothes, and we have to vacuum everything. And we have to wash our hands after touching *anything*. Otherwise they come back and you have to do it all over again."

"You can't be serious."

"I don't want lice in this house." My wife is half-German, so obsessive cleanliness is her birthright. "Go to CVS and see if you can find a shampoo. And a comb. They make special lice combs."

My daughter, meanwhile, was staring up at us with increasing alarm. "Do I have bugs in my hair?"

My wife knelt down. "Honey, we're doing everything

we can to make sure you don't have bugs in your hair, and that they don't get anywhere else in the house. Okay?"

"Okay."

I hopped in the car and drove at light speed to the nearest drugstore. The lice shampoos were on the bottom shelf in the skin care section, tucked away from prying eyes. I tried to buy the most serious-looking one I could find. There was one called RID, with a logo shaped like a stop sign. That seemed very stern to me. Also, there was a comb included free with the shampoo, all for fifteen bucks. So I grabbed the kit along with a bag of chips. I never ran an errand without properly rewarding myself.

When I returned home, my wife was just getting off the phone with the doctor, one of superstar Dr. Ferris's satellite pediatricians. She had taken copious notes during the call. It looked as if she had taken down enough information to launch a Mars probe.

I took out the lice removal kit and showed it to her, beaming with pride.

"The comb came free!" I said proudly.

"Oh, that shampoo's no good."

"It isn't?"

"It's a pesticide. Look at the label."

I looked at the label and checked the FAQ on the website. My wife was right. You had to ventilate the room before using the shampoo. You could not touch the shampoo. You could not eat the shampoo. There were enough warnings on the label to make you think you were handling a chemical weapon. I looked at the reviews for the shampoo on Amazon (which I should have done prior to jumping in my car, but I really wanted some chips), and the reviews averaged two stars. You could sell a baby snuff film on Amazon and still get their reviewers to throw you four stars, but this shampoo was not only poisonous but also ineffective. One review headline said "USELESS" and nothing else.

"Jesus, this stuff is horrible," I said.

"The doctor has a shampoo we can use."

"So what's it called? I'll go back."

"No, she literally has it. She has it left over from when one of her kids got it. A comb too. She said you could go to her house and grab it, but you have to go now, before she goes to bed."

I had never had a doctor extend such a courtesy. "She's okay with me going to her home?"

"Yeah, isn't that incredible?"

"I better go before she realizes that she just broke the fourth wall. The rest of doctordom will never forgive her."

"When you get back," my wife said, "we have to check you."

"What do you mean, we have to check me?"

"The whole house is compromised. We have to check everyone, including you and me."

"Pfft. I don't have lice."

"You don't know that. You could have given it to her."

"How dare you!" I said. "For all we know, *you* could have given it to *her*!"

"You don't always shampoo at the gym."

"Well, sometimes YOU shower at night. They could jump in your hair during the day and have hours to have hot lice sex with one another. Just because you're a girl doesn't mean you're so immaculate."

And then my head itched. I tried to avoid scratching it because I didn't want my wife's theory proven that instant. The itch grew and grew and grew until it felt as if there were a giant louse perched atop my head, rubbing his greasy exoskeleton all over me. I caved in and scratched my head.

"This is not a lice scratch," I said. "Just one of my many normal, daily itches."

My wife handed me a dishrag. "Cover the headrest in your car with this. Otherwise they can embed themselves in the headrest and lay eggs."

"No, they can't."

"Yes, they can. We're gonna have to vacuum the mini-van too. You gotta run now. That doctor is waiting for you."

I got back into the car and laid the dishrag over my headrest. I felt the itch on my scalp again but tried my best to ignore it. I even turned the radio up because I thought it would help distract me. But the itch was there. It was *alive*. It was screaming and yelling at me to address it, to give it the recognition it wanted. *I can't have lice. I shower every day. It's just dandruff. Jusssst dandruff. And if it's just dandruff, why then I'd be a fool NOT to scratch it!* So I did. I scratched the shit out of my head for a solid mile.

I got to the doctor's house and she greeted me at the door in her nightgown and I did my best to not look directly at her because I felt like I was intruding on sacred ground. She gave me the shampoo and the comb and I thanked her over and over again, as if she had just given me a check for a billion dollars. *Oh, thank you, thank you. I can't believe how nice this was of you. You don't know how much this means to our family. And I know you have a life and a house of your own and you didn't even charge me a co-pay for it and that is arguably the greatest thing one person has ever done for another and I AM FOREVER IN YOUR DEBT.*

I raced home with the precious lice-killing kit. The next morning, we stripped every sheet, washed every stitch of clothing, and vacuumed every square inch of the house. We even washed the covers of the couch cushions. My wife set our daughter up in a wooden chair with a little smock tied around her neck. She put on dishwasher gloves and applied the shampoo to the girl's scalp, making sure every strand was lovingly coated in fancy *organic* poison. Then she took the comb, which looked like two dozen steel sewing needles bunched tightly together, and went through the hair handful by handful, pulling out COLONIES of lice and showing them to our daughter.

"Was that in my hair?" the girl asked.

"Yes," my wife said.

"COOL!"

"No, not cool. Ew."

"Ew."

It was painstaking work, and the girl sat there, miraculously, for nearly two hours without complaint.

"You are being so good," my wife told her. "After this, you can have anything you want."

"Even a car?" she asked.

"Not a car, no."

The whole time I watched my wife disinfect her, all I could think was *oh shit, I hope I don't have it*.

"Did you check him?" my wife asked me, pointing to our son.

"Oh, right," I said. I ran over to the boy and spent exactly half a second running my fingers through his hair. "Nope! Looks good."

"Drew, you have to *look*."

I looked again while the boy twisted and squirmed away from me.

"Deddy, no!" he shouted.

"Lemme just check you." I parted his hair every which way, peeking through the blond curls and praying that I'd find nothing but white scalp. But there was a nit. And another nit. And then three. There weren't anywhere near as many as there were in the girl's hair, but they were there. The little egg capsules were unmistakable.

"Does he have it?" my wife asked me.

"Uh, well, he kinda does. Not all the way like her. Just a few here and there. Maybe that's okay."

"I gotta treat his hair too."

"Crap."

I sat idly by and watched my wife painstakingly remove the nits from our son's scalp while he brayed and screamed like a captive animal. When the day of tireless lice eradication was at last all over, the kids went to sleep and it was time for the final examination.

"Who examines who first?" I asked.

"Do me first," my wife said. "Then I'll do you."

"This is *soooooooo* sexy."

"Let's just get it over with."

She turned around and I teased out small bunches of hair at a time, making a sincere effort to look for the lice, applying a jeweler's eye to the tens of thousands of roots and follicles. I found nothing. But I didn't want my wife to think that I was half-assing the search, so I checked her scalp three, four times over.

"I don't think there's anything here," I said. "And I'm not saying that because I'm lazy. I really don't think you have it."

"Are you sure?" she asked. I could tell she wanted to believe it.

"There's nothing here. I think you're good."

Now it was my turn. I presented myself for inspection, shutting my eyes and silently hoping that I wouldn't end up sitting in the Lice Chair for two hours.

"I can't find anything," she said, and I heaved a sigh of relief. But neither of us was 100 percent convinced. Before bed, we both shampooed our hair thrice over. When we lay down to sleep after all of the driving and combing and vacuuming, the specter of the lice still lingered.

"Who do you think gave it to her?" my wife asked.

"I don't know. Someone gave it to her. She didn't get it

herself. She's a very clean little girl. Someone rotten and filthy transmitted it."

"Do you think it was one of the neighborhood kids?"

I began ranking all the kids at her bus stop in order of cleanliness.

"We took her to a playground," I said. "Maybe she got it there. Maybe we shouldn't go back."

"Maybe we should warn other people."

"Maybe that playground is one giant biohazard. Remember the pudding shorts?"

"I actually read online tonight that lice prefer clean girls' hair because it's long."

"Really? So, in a way, having lice is actually a sign of *good* hygiene."

"Definitely."

"Totally."

I had now shifted from being a cruel judge of the lice-ridden to one of their more passionate advocates. *How dare anyone think my child is dirty simply because she has lice? No one better tease her.* I realized that obsessing over the source of the lice had turned me into a paranoid lunatic. The truth is that getting lice has virtually nothing to do with cleanliness and everything to do with bad luck, and the lengths to which you must go to eliminate lice serve as proof of just how durable the little fuckers are.

The itch on my scalp came back. *Oh God. What if I really do have it? What if the lice were dormant until now and are beginning to lay their eggs inside my pillow? What if I open my mouth when I'm sleeping and they shit into my throat? What if they crawl down to my dick? CRABS. I'll have crabs. I'll have crabs and I wouldn't even have gotten the pleasure of making love to a stripper in order to contract them.*

The itching spread. I scratched my neck. I scratched my ear. I scratched my elbow. Soon my wife began scratching everything as well: her face, her legs, her underarms. Imaginary lice had washed over us, skittering around our bodies and infiltrating every nook of the house. Nowhere was safe. We would never rid ourselves of them. The entire house would have to be burned down and rebuilt from scratch. Our minivan would have to be traded in, and we'd have to face the ethical dilemma of whether to tell the dealer that our car was a receptacle for indestructible vermin. Our lives would never, ever be the same.

Morning broke and I found that, despite my growing paranoia, I had managed to fall asleep. My wife arose and sprinted to our kids' room to check the sheets in the bunk beds. She plucked a single living louse from the pillowcase on the top bunk and held it up.

"Another one!" she cried out.

"What does that mean?" I asked.

"It means we clean everything again."

"NOOOOOOOOOOOOOO . . ."

My daughter went to lie down on the carpet and my wife quickly reprimanded her.

"Don't put your head on anything."

"I can't put my head on the floor?" she asked.

"No, you can't touch anything with your head all day."

We washed the sheets and vacuumed the mattresses and

went through the shampoo-and-combing process a second, awful time. By the time my wife had finished the job, there wasn't a trace of lice to be found anywhere in the house. No bugs. No nits. I took the lice that my wife had combed out and carefully shook them into a plastic bag, then disposed of them outside, where they could never menace us again. Gradually, a feeling of normalcy returned to the house.

"I think you got them all," I told my wife.

"I think I did too."

"You could do this for a living. You could be the Lice Fixer."

"They have a lady like that here. She's called the Lice Lady. You pay her three hundred dollars and she gets rid of the lice in your kid's hair for you."

"Ewwww! There must be lice all over her house."

"Yeah. Disgusting."

As the days went on, the lice threat slowly faded from view. The couch and the rug and the children's hair remained spotless. But sometimes, in the middle of the night, I get a little itch. I think about the possibility of a single nit that we missed somewhere, hiding inside a shoe, or in a curtain, or tucked in the folds of a bathroom towel. It's lying dormant, waiting for the right time to hatch, the right time to bust out and find a scalp to nest in, to start a new family of blood-thirsty little fuckers that will stop at nothing until my house and my family have been ruined. It's waiting for me. I know it. Then again, maybe it left here and is out in the world, ready to find a new host. Maybe it's found *you*.

THE LIST

There was a list and I never deviated from the list. It had eggs, milk, yogurt, cheese, meat, cereal, vegetables, and fruit. Too much fruit, too many vegetables: bananas, three different kinds of berries, apples, oranges, lettuce, carrots, peppers, parsley, and more. I was in the minivan, scouting the list, and I knew right away that it demanded way too much time in the produce section. It was always my mission to get in and out of the grocery store as quickly as possible. One time, I made it to the store and back home in just thirty-eight minutes with both kids in tow. I was determined to beat that record, but the more time I spent in the produce section picking and weighing shit while two hundred old people milled about groping for Fuji apples, the more likely it was that I would fail.

I had two coupons in my back pocket that my wife said

I should use at the register to save money. But I considered those coupons an optional luxury. Using coupons meant that I would have to rely on a clerk to scan them, and that one of the coupons would inevitably scan wrong, and that the manager would be called in, and that I would be stuck in that store for nine years. It wasn't worth saving thirty cents on a box of orzo if I couldn't beat the record.

There were four options for handling the children at the store. I could get one of those mammoth carts that were shaped like fire trucks and strap both kids into the cab up front. But those things were vile. They took up too much space in the aisle, and grocery store managers always made sure to litter every aisle with four hundred stand-alone displays for Cajun seasoning that were just wide enough to destroy traffic flow. It should be legal to take your cart and blast straight through these displays, as if they were fruit carts in a movie car chase. Also, the fire truck carts never had enough room for actual food. And my children always wanted to get out of them halfway through.

Another option was to put my son in a regular cart and let my daughter roam free. This never worked because my son would see my daughter waltzing around freely and realize that he was getting a raw deal. I could also let both kids roam free, but that usually ended with them having a slap fight in the freezer aisle. Instead, my strategy was to let them push around the little green kiddie carts provided by our store while I went about the business of actual shopping. My kids went running for the kiddie cart section as I grabbed a self-scanner. All the kiddie carts were taken.

"There are no carts!" my daughter said.

"You guys can hang on the side of my cart," I said. Now, this was a horrible thing to suggest. There are diagrams all over every shopping cart that tell you to not do this. The girl had a penchant for hanging off the front of the cart and then jumping off as it was rolling forward, allowing the cart to break both her ankles quickly and efficiently. But time was of the essence, so I grasped for the quickest and easiest possible solution. No way I was gonna get a fire truck cart.

Then, by the grace of God, a store worker came by with two green kiddie carts for my kids.

"Thank you so much," I said to him. I turned to my kids. "What do you guys say to the nice man for giving us these great carts?"

My son looked up at him and shouted out, "WHAT'S UP, FUCKFACE?!"

He had just watched a Thomas the Tank Engine DVD where someone says something that sounds like "WHAT'S UP, FUCKFACE?!" but is *not* "WHAT'S UP, FUCK-FACE?!" But when my son repeated it, it sounded very much like "WHAT'S UP, FUCKFACE?!" I bent down and looked my son in the eye.

"No, no, no. We don't say that. I know you're not trying to say anything bad, but it sounds like something bad."

"WHAT'S UP, FUCKFAY?!"

The nice store worker walked away, unfazed. He was clearly used to children shouting random crap inside the store.

"Seriously, what is it that you're saying?" I asked my son. " 'What's up, Front Case?' "

"WUZZOUT, FUCKFACE?!"

Other shoppers began to stare.

"You know what? Let's just move along."

The children began fighting over who got to use the first green cart.

"I want it!" the girl screamed.

"Me too!" said the boy.

"They're the same cart!" I said. "Do you not see this? There is literally no difference between these carts. They are the SAME."

"I want it!" she said.

"WHAT'S UP, FUCKFACE?!"

"I'm leaving to go shopping," I said. "You two can jolly well sort this out yourselves." This is what you have to do as a parent. You have to let the kids fight it out or else they'll constantly look to you to solve their disputes and then bitch about the way you solved them.

Eventually, the two kids sorted it out and came trailing behind me. I got a text from my wife asking me to also get half-and-half for her coffee. I texted her back that I would and then instantly forgot that I had to get it. If it wasn't written on the list, it was doomed.

I went to the deli first because the deli takes forever and my kids wanted ham. I tried using the digital ordering kiosk but it was broken because of course it was fucking broken. God forbid the most convenient amenity of the entire market be operational. Both my kids came running up with their carts and took thirty numbers each from the electronic deli number dispenser. We were next in line behind an old woman who was buying an eighth of a pound of everything in the case. I redirected my children to the produce section, got everything on the list, went back to the deli, and by this time my children were so starved for lunch meat that I was prepared to cut off a shank of my own thigh, cure it in brine, and feed it to them.

Finally, the deli guy called one of our sixty numbers. He gave us our pound of ham and I quickly handed slices to my kids, who then promptly dropped their slices, picked them up off the floor, and ate them. While they were eating filthy, germ-ridden floor ham, I double-checked the list to make sure I had no reason to go back to the produce section, because the produce section was worse than South Sudan. We were good. I still had twenty-seven minutes to work with.

"We've got all our fruits and veggies. LET'S GO, DUDES," I said.

We got away from the deli and the produce section. The next thing on the list was a box of organic alphabet cookies. I had no idea where they were. They could have been anywhere. They could have been in the cookie aisle. They could have been in the natural foods aisle. They could have been located merely in my wife's imagination. I scoured the aisles, searching for the box while trying to keep an eye on both children, who were now openly racing their little green carts up and down the aisles. I came by a box of organic alphabet cookies, but they were CINNAMON and not VANILLA. Would that matter? Would my children, who were pickier about food than a dying Steve Jobs was, notice the difference and cry? Or was it better to get credit for securing everything on the list? *Fuck it.* In they went.

I ticked off the other items: the sugar and flour and cereal and chicken. Seventeen minutes left to break the record. So close I could taste it. My daughter asked for a bag of potato chips and I relented.

"Can we open them now?" she asked.

"I have to buy them. Then we can open them."

"But you took that Coke and opened it and drank it."

"That's different because I'm a grown-up."

I had three more items left: cheese sticks, yogurt, and milk. I checked the list again just to make sure I wasn't wrong. We were nearly done and nothing traumatic had happened. We hauled ass to the dairy aisle and I looked at the yogurt. There were fifty-seven different varieties: tubs and tubes and little four-packs of Greek yogurt, Dannon yogurt, whipped yogurt, plain yogurt, and Danimals, which are not actually yogurt but rather yogurt-like drinks forged from buffalo drippings. I was baffled. All the list said was "yogurt," which was bullshit. It may as well have said, "GUESS THE YOGURT ASSHOLE HAHAHAHA."

I grabbed the first tub of vanilla yogurt I saw, then the cheese sticks and the milk, and we were done. Twelve more minutes to go. We could still break the record.

I got to the SCAN IT! line and there was one person in front of me who was clearly using his little scanner for the first time and was in need of assistance. But he didn't go looking for help. He just stood there, waiting for the magic grocery store fairies to appear to solve the mysteries of the self-checkout for him. He had enough groceries to survive a bioterrorist attack.

My kids began to mentally break down while waiting in line. They had yet to understand the concept of lines. *Why do we have to wait? Who are these other people? Can't they just die? This isn't fair.* They began pushing their carts into each other and crying. I told them to stop. Then my son rammed me with his cart.

"Please don't hit Daddy with the cart. You guys are doing such a great job right now and I'm so proud of you, but now Daddy's shins are bruised and he's losing valuable time. Can you help me out here? Can you wait patiently?"

"Oat-kay."

My daughter pointed at the candy display and gave me her best "I'm smiling because I want something" smile.

"Can I have some gum?"

"Yes," I said. I didn't want to fight. You could have offered to sever my finger to speed up the process and I would have agreed. It's like an innocent man breaking down and confessing after eight hours of relentless interrogation. I wish I could have just settled down and enjoyed the time I had with my kids no matter where we were, to not treat excursions like this as one more goddamn obstacle in the way of getting the day over with. But I couldn't. The people around me were less people than they were faceless enemy combatants. Giving myself some arbitrary time record to break was my only way of turning it into a sport instead of a grueling ordeal to be endured. When you're single, you don't think twice about going to the store. It's nothing. But for someone with kids in tow, it's an *expedition*. It requires planning and equipment and detailed strategies. It's as daunting as a paralyzed man attempting to dress himself.

My daughter pointed at a small bag of sour cream and onion chips.

"Can we have those chips too?"

In they went.

"And can we have some M&M's?"

In they went.

"And can we have some Golden Oreos?"

In they went. Ten minutes left. Every minute you wait in line at a grocery store takes four hours in perceived time. It's like being high.

Finally, the amateur in front of us was finished and I whipped out my scanner to show the rest of the store how checking out was done. Everyone was gonna be in awe of my speed at the register. Managers would salute me. The deli guy would hand me bonus ham.

But my scanner thingy didn't work. The cashier needed the key. Why she couldn't have had the register key on her at all times was beyond me. Eight minutes left. Hope was fading. I double-checked the list one final time and saw the word "STAMPS" in block letters surrounded by a tasteful double border. Stamps were easy to forget because they came at the end of the grocery run, after the main items on the list were already obtained. I was not in the mood for stamps. *Fuck those stamps.*

We finally had everything paid for and bagged and I got the kids back across the Parking Lot of Death and into the car. The girl demanded her gum and I tore through the packaging with my teeth to get her a stick of Trident as quickly as possible.

"You guys were amazing," I told them. "We CRUSHED that trip. We SLAYED it. We CRUSHSLAYED it. Now hold on to your butts because I'm driving fast all the way home."

I spied the clock and had a scant six minutes to go. The idea of getting across town that quickly was foolhardy. But screw that. I would get home under the wire and have my record and the whole world would bow at my feet. We were going to do it. The record was *mine*.

Then I pulled out of my spot and a ninety-year-old woman in a Crown Victoria blocked the way for ten minutes.

"Guhhhhhhhh."

"Dad, that woman is blocking the way," said my daughter. "And that's not fair!"

"No, it isn't."

"Can I have more gum?"

"No."

We broke free and when I finally got home, I began to unload the bags and bring them into the kitchen, dejected but proud of the children for helping with the effort. *We'll get them next time, by God.* Once the last bag was inside, it was all over. No more store. Not for a few days, at least. My wife began sorting through everything.

"This isn't the right yogurt," she said. "And where's the half-and-half? And the stamps? Did you use the coupons? Why did you buy Golden Oreos?"

"Because I earned them."

"WHAT'S UP, FUCKFACE?!"

FUNLAND

We went to the beach for a week, even though going to the beach is a horrible idea when you have children. It's hot, and expensive, and you have to pack so much shit that you may as well hire a Mayflower truck. But my wife couldn't stand the idea of spending an entire summer inside the same home, staring at the same walls, driving on the same roads. Do it long enough and you come down with a kind of expanded cabin fever, encompassing anything within a five-mile radius. So off we went.

Rehoboth Beach, Delaware, is like a lot of East Coast beach towns. There are bars and ice cream parlors and little tiny surf shops that people crowd into to soak in a little bit of air-conditioning and peruse T-shirts with tired *Anchorman* quotes. There's a wide boardwalk that you can stroll along to gawk at all the white beach trash: four-hundred-pound people in tank tops, women with torso-length tattoos of the Pittsburgh Steelers logo, shoeless children, etc. The main attraction along this boardwalk is Funland, an amusement park with rides that vary in quality from "second-tier Six Flags ride that you get on because the roller coaster line is too long" down to "loosely bolted gypsy carnie death trap at the Allendale County Pig Show." The kids were intent on going to Funland every day. They didn't want to go to the beach. They didn't want to sit in a restaurant and eat, like, food. All they wanted was Funland. Funland was the goal. Funland Funland Funland.

We arrived at my in-laws' modest town house in nearby Dewey at around 4:00 P.M. I asked the kids if they wanted to go out for dinner.

"FUNLAND!"

I told them that it might be a little late for Funland, so maybe we should wait until—

"FUNLAND!"

"Well, what about the beach?" I asked.

"FUNLAND!"

"So, I guess you two want to go to Funland."

"FUNLAND!"

"All right. Let's go."

My wife grew concerned. "Honey, it's getting late for them."

"Oh, come on," I said. "We're on vacation. We're supposed to loosen up. Let them enjoy themselves." Secretly, I had no issue with us going to Funland because there was an ice cream store a block away from Funland that had Peanut

Butter Tastykake ice cream, and I wanted it. I wanted to swim in it.

We all hopped in the car and drove to the boardwalk. I found a parking spot that was roughly the same distance to Funland as the house we were staying in. I got the kids out and we began to march in the lethal July heat toward the park of their dreams. By the fourth block, the kids were noticeably dragging. My son asked me to pick him up. I carried him five feet and then put him back down because my back hurt. We passed by a row of shaggy rental houses, each one designed to house the maximum allowable number of drunken twentysomethings. I saw them all out on their rickety patios, blasting music and drinking cocktails out of plastic Solo cups. I used to do that sort of thing. God, that was fun. I wanted to run into one of the houses, down G-and-Ts by the fistful, do five bong rips, and then pass out on a filthy mattress in the basement.

My daughter caught sight of a giant dragon's head rising over the houses and immediately screamed with joy.

"That's Funland!" she cried out. "That's the Sea Dragon!"

"Is dat Funlann, Deddy?" asked my son.

"Yeah," I said. "I think we're close, guys."

We staggered into the park and both kids went sprinting for their preferred rides. The boy went with my wife over to a set of miniature cars that drove around in a tight circle, while the girl got in line immediately for the Sea Dragon: a giant Viking ship that went back and forth, higher and higher, until it was nearly upside down. It didn't go all the way around, which was good. When I was a kid, I went to an old amusement park in Minnesota that had a ship that went all the way around. You could see the wallets and spare change and vomit raining down whenever it hung in midair.

I went to the ticket booth, threw down a twenty, jammed the ticket book into my sweaty shorts pocket, and rushed to join the girl at the front of the Sea Dragon line. We took a seat at the back of the ship (cost: five tickets each). I craned my head, trying to locate my son and my wife. But the ride started and I gave up my efforts because watching the girl's face as we went higher and higher was such a joy. The ship cleared the rooftops and now we could see the beach, the ocean, and the surrounding towns. The higher we went, the harder she laughed. I made sure to play the victim for her.

"Whoa, hey!" I screamed. "You didn't tell me it was gonna go THIS high! This is too high! GAHHH!"

"AHAHAHAHAHAHA!"

Sixty seconds later, the ship settled back down on the ground and the girl demanded another ride, and then another. There was barely a line at this point, so we were able to take as many consecutive trips as we pleased. By the eighth time, I was seasick and begged her to spare me from another ride.

"I'm not joking this time," I said. "I'll die if we do that again. I have vertigo now."

"More, more, more!"

"I'm gonna switch with Mom and she's gonna take you. She hates rides like this, so you're probably gonna end up playing in the arcade. Can you deal with that?"

"Okay."

We went in search of my wife and found her watching my son whiz around on the giant swing. After a mere half an hour at Funland, our clothes were soaked through with sweat and the children could barely keep their heads above their necks. But children will never readily acknowledge their own tiredness. Nothing pisses them off more than telling them, "Hey, you look tired!" They'll claw your face off if you tell them that. It wounds their pride. You just have to let them run themselves ragged until they collapse from near-fatal levels of dehydration and exhaustion. My kids wanted to stay at Funland, so I cut them a deal.

"Listen," I said. "One more ride, and then we go home for French fries and ice cream. I'm not even gonna pretend that you'll eat the other things I put on your dinner plate. Just fries and then ice cream. Deal?"

Both nodded their heads vigorously. The girl took off to the arcade with my wife and I went with the boy to find his own last hurrah. Toward the back of the park, behind a small track where little trucks scooted around for the relatively high price of three tickets, there was the Jungle: a massive, Rube Goldberg–style obstacle course where kids entered through one cube and battled through a series of rope bridges and slides and ball pits and ladders until they emerged out of another cube six months later. It was cool as shit. I wanted to go into it myself. You weren't allowed to wear shoes inside this toddler matrix. You had to place them in a little cubby and then let your parents watch in horror as your feet grew blacker and blacker with each progressive step.

I looked at my son. He was three years old. A robust three. A remarkably stubborn three. There wasn't a trace of insincerity to him. I looked into his big Tweety Bird eyes and knew that he was going into this thing whether I liked it or not.

"I don't think I have enough tickets for this one," I told him.

"I wand to bo in dere."

"You sure you can handle it?"

"Wes!"

"All right. Last ride."

I plunked down the tickets, slipped off the boy's shoes, and watched him burrow into the entrance. He climbed up through a plastic flap to the second level of the Jungle and jumped into a plastic ball pit. The balls were ancient. You could see the geologic buildup of dried snot that had accumulated on them over the course of time, layer after layer of petrified boogers. He struggled to wade through the pit, as if trapped in quicksand. I shouted encouragement to him: "You're okay! You're doing just great!"

But that was merely a taste of what the Jungle had in store for him. After the ball pit, he had to climb up another level. The cubes were just high enough for this to be a struggle for him. I watched as he reached through the plastic flap and tried to pull himself further up. It took him a while and I offered him a way out by shouting, "You can turn around! You don't have to do the whole thing!" But he ignored me and pressed on, hoisting himself up and coming to a long rope bridge, with an opening between each step wide enough for his entire leg to fall through. The boy stepped cautiously as older kids swarmed around and past him, and he looked genuinely surprised that none of them stopped to help.

Ever cross a rope bridge with no shoes on? Don't. The rope digs into your arches and you quickly find yourself in agonizing discomfort. I could see it in my son's face as he walked gingerly across. He knew he had gotten in way over his head. Now he was beginning to cry because he hated the Jungle and there was no way out of it. It was his own private 'Nam. I kept waiting for a ten-year-old to grab him and scream, "You know where you are? You're in the Jungle, baby! YOU'RE GONNA DIEEEEEE!"

There were only two ways out: down the way he came, or up several more levels to a tunnel slide that would bring him, conceivably, back down to the exit without much fuss (or pudding). But the climb up to that slide now appeared as daunting as summiting K2, and I begged my son to turn around.

"It's not worth it!" I shouted.

The big kids were passing him and he hated the idea of looking like the one kid who couldn't handle what the Jungle was throwing at him. He kept climbing upward. He slipped out of view for a moment and I couldn't pinpoint his location. I was afraid the Jungle had swallowed him whole. I imagined a trapdoor hidden inside the maze that sent unwitting toddlers down to a special carny dungeon, where they would be set aside for meat. Then he emerged out of a tunnel and was nearly as high as the Sea Dragon at its peak swing. But he couldn't see the tunnel slide. He didn't know there was a way out. He grabbed the netting and began crying loud enough for everyone to hear.

"DEDDY!"

I went over to the Jungle's operator, a sixteen-year-old who almost certainly took the job strictly for weed money.

"Is there any other way out of this thing?" I asked.

He shrugged. Actually, to call it a shrug is an insult to shrugs because the garden-variety shrug takes at least some physical effort. He just shrugged with his face. I looked at the entrance of the structure and I tried to see if I could fit through the flap to get to my son, but it was hopeless. Only a very small Chinese acrobat could have contorted himself into such a tight space. I backed away from the Jungle and stared up at the boy, who was still crying.

"Okay, be cool!" I shouted. "I'm gonna talk you down! But you have to do exactly as I say. Okay?"

"Oat-kay."

I assumed the role of police negotiator, talking a suicidal man off a ledge. "There is a slide that will take you down to me. Just follow the big kids."

The boy ignored my advice and swam against the current.

"No, no, no!" I shouted. "That's the wrong way!" I wanted to prove to everyone around that I was an excellent negotiator. But my son continued back where he came from, fighting back tears along the way. He didn't want the big kids to see him crying anymore. I changed course and started guiding him through the way back to the entrance, even though he clearly knew where he was going. He lowered himself back down through a handful of cubes.

"There's a rope bridge coming up. You're going to have to cross it," I said. He arrived at the bridge and while the big kids didn't help him across, they at least had the common courtesy to get out of the way. Usually, big kids just run through smaller children as if they're blocks to kick over. He went across the painful steps and paused once in a while to look at me, his face hot and swollen. I wanted to pole-vault up to him and kiss every part of his head, but I was helpless to aid him. He'd have to make it on his own, and I would have to watch the struggle unfold in real time.

He got to the end of the bridge and then lowered himself down to the second level. "Yes, yes!" I said. "Keep going! I believe in you!" Exhausted, he came to the ball pit and fell into it, like a triathlete collapsing at the finish line. This final obstacle was nearly too much for him. It was Shackleton's trek across South Georgia Island. But now he was low enough that I could speak to him directly through the netting.

"You're almost there. You can do it, little guy. Get up and wade through those balls. Wade, damn you!"

The boy slowly picked himself up and carried himself across. There was a final hole to fall into and as he slipped through the flap down to safety, I scooped him up and wrapped his legs around me and tucked his big blond head into my neck and kissed him over and over again.

"You're all right," I said to him. "You're safe now, fella."

He was stuttering through tears. "D-d-d-d-deddy, I wand to bo home."

"We're going home right now. I promise."

Just then, my wife showed up with my daughter. The girl stared up at the Jungle and shrieked with delight.

"I wanna go in THAT!" she said.

My son saw the look on his sister's face, then wriggled out of my arms and seemed to find a second wind, looking as if we had just arrived at Funland this instant. I knew what he was gonna say before he even said it.

"Don't say it," I begged him.

"ME TOO!"

Shit.

PIZZA NIGHT

We made pizza every week because the two kids subsisted on Kraft Mac and pizza and virtually nothing else. You can do everything right and still not succeed in getting your kids to eat properly. You can cook all your own meals. You can avoid McDonald's and warn the children that eating at McDonald's will make them fat and diseased. You can threaten to withhold dessert if they don't eat half a zucchini cube. You can do all those things and still end up with a child who refuses to eat anything other than chicken nuggets assembled from fire-hosed penis meat.

One time, I bought my daughter a cheeseburger and begged her to eat it, to just take one bite, and when she did take a nibble I was THRILLED. I was ecstatic over her eating a cheeseburger, which is stupid because a cheeseburger is pure shit. The bun is shit. The patty is shit. The cheese is shit. Every element of it belongs to the FDA-labeled Shit Group. But it was something different, and I had reached a point where anything different was acceptable. She spit out the bite. I ate the rest of the cheeseburger because I'm a responsible person and I owed it to all the starving malaria babies of the world.

Pizza was the one thing that we could eat regularly as a family without me worrying about the kids being ungrateful little bastards and literally bursting into tears at the prospect of eating a nice meal that dared to include things like rice or steak. It was the most reliable way to avoid dinnertime confrontation, with the children angrily pushing their plates away and me getting pissed at the kids for pushing their plates away. Pizza was the uniter. Pizza kept us together.

So I threw myself into making the best homemade pizza I possibly could. None of that "put some Ragú on a Boboli shell" crap. No, no, if I was making pizza at home, it was gonna be BADASS. I tried making my own dough, which caused the whole house to smell like a warm yeast infection. Then I experimented with store-bought dough and found that Safeway's was the best. I learned how to stretch the dough without tearing it. I would dust the counter in flour and let the wad of dough fall away from its plastic bag and plop down onto the counter. Then I would push the dough down and work it with the butt of my palms, taking special care not to press down too hard. Then I would pick the dough up and let gravity stretch it out some more, running the edges between my thumb and forefinger all the way around and getting it so thin that it was practically a sheet of molecules. I pictured myself as an Italian immigrant running my own pizza parlor in some nameless section of Queens, yelling at neighborhood kids to stop playing stickball outside my storefront. *Yousa kids-a, stop making-a trouble. It's-a me, Mario!*

I found all the best ingredients to use on top: San Marzano tomatoes pureed in a blender, fresh mozzarella cheese, dried oregano, freshly grated Parmigiano-Reggiano (not that Kraft garbage that comes in a green can), torn-up basil leaves, pepperoni, and a little drizzle of olive oil. In time, I became a master pizzaiolo. I would go to pizza restaurants and immediately declare the pie we ordered stale dogshit compared to my own. I dreamed of celebrity chefs coming to my house and pronouncing my pie the finest in the world. *How does he do it using only a gas oven?* I became unreasonably excited whenever Pizza Night came around. I would spend the workday brainstorming new toppings. *What if I put an entire Caesar salad on top of a sausage pizza? Would that be so wrong?* The idea of making pizza and seeing the kids actually enjoying it and me drinking an entire bottle of wine and eating half a bag of pepperoni while cooking it brought me to near-autoerotic levels of anticipation. Pizza Night was king.

One day, I came back from the store with all the pizza ingredients and I walked in on the kids watching TV.

"Do you know what tonight is?" I asked them.

They kept staring at the TV.

"It's Pizza Night, people!"

Both kids screamed out "YAY." My daughter jumped up and did a little dance.

"Yes, yes, that's it!" I cried. "DO YOUR PIZZA DANCE."

"Can I help you make the pizza?" she asked.

"Uh . . . are you sure?"

"Yeah."

"Yeah, of course you can."

"Cool!"

I grabbed my dirty Minnesota Vikings apron and preheated the oven to 450 degrees. The girl ran to her little play kitchen and grabbed a plastic toy rolling pin.

"I'm gonna roll the dough!" she said.

"Yes, you can help with that," I said. "Now the important thing to remember is to not tear the dough. If we tear the dough, then Pizza Night is ruined forever."

"Really?"

"No. Just don't rip the dough."

"Okay."

I floured the counter and let the dough plop down. The girl pulled a little wooden ladybug stool up next to me and jammed her rolling pin into the mess of dough on the counter.

"Wait!" I said. "You have to flour the pin!"

"I do?"

"It's very crucial."

But it was too late. The pin had fastened itself to the dough and every time the girl rolled it, it stuck to the pin and came apart, destroying the dough's precious integrity.

"Wait, we need to start over," I said.

"No, we don't. It's easy," she said.

"Take the pin out. You gotta take the pin out of the dough. You know what? Let me do the dough and then you can spread the sauce."

I commandeered the pin from her and tossed it into the sink, then began stretching the dough with my hands, working feverishly to undo the damage.

"See how I do this?" I asked. "Isn't this fun?"

The girl now looked bored. "Yeah, sure." She started to wander back to the TV and I quickly put the dough down on the cookie sheet so that I could restrain her.

"Wait, wait," I said. "I'm done stretching the dough. See? Now you can spread the sauce."

"Really?"

"Yes, really. I swear. I won't interfere."

She got back up on her little stool and I presented her with a container of sauce. She dipped her spoon in it and spattered it all over the counter. I interfered.

"Sweetie, you have to spread it evenly. Try not to get it on the counter."

"I know! I got it."

"Yes, but you're spattering it, see?"

I took her hand and tried spreading the sauce with her, like a golf instructor helping you with your grip. I was the one doing the real spreading. I was simply treating her hand as an extension of the spoon.

"See? Isn't this fun?" I asked her.

She wrenched away from my grip. "No! I wanna do it!"

"Okay, but just please try to keep it contained to the dough itself."

She spattered the sauce again.

"Oops! Sorry," she said.

"That's okay," I said. But I was lying. She was ruining the pizza. "Maybe we should take turns spreading the sauce."

"No! I can do it." And she spattered the sauce yet again. I grabbed the spoon back.

"Okay, you're fired from this."

"Aw."

"Lemme spread this sauce and you can put the cheese on. You'd be good at that."

"Okay."

I spread the sauce lovingly around, bringing it right to the edge of the dough without spilling it over the side, finishing up just as she was wandering back to the TV again.

"Cheese time!" I said. "You can do the cheese now."

"Okay," she said.

Right then, my wife walked in.

"Oooh, are you guys making pizza together?"

"We are," I said. "We're having tons of fun, right?"

The girl said nothing.

"You're letting her help, right, Drew?" my wife asked.

"Absolutely. She helped roll the dough."

"No, I didn't," the girl said.

"And she helped spread the sauce."

"No, I didn't."

"Of course you did. I did virtually nothing."

"You have to let her help," my wife said. "It's okay if she makes mistakes."

"I know, I know. I'm letting her put the cheese on it, I swear."

My wife and I had just bought a parenting book called *Love and Logic* that said you need to let kids do as many things on their own as humanly possible. That way, they become confident and more self-reliant and, most important, they don't bother you with whiny bullshit all day long. Self-reliant kids are the ones that end up building railroads and annexing small Baltic nations. If you constantly hover and do everything for your kids, you hinder their maturation process. They become convinced that they *need* you to do everything for them. The authors argued that if you let children make mistakes when they're young, the cost of those mistakes is relatively low: a spilled milk glass, a missed school bus ride, etc. Those are mistakes that any parent can live with. But if you butt in at every opportunity, then the child makes much more costly mistakes later in life: committing armed robbery, shooting liquefied crack into her eyeballs, going to law school, etc.

So here was a perfect opportunity for me to let my child stand there and make mistakes with relatively little consequence. I had jumped in when she screwed up the dough. I had jumped in when she got tomato sauce all over everything. If I jumped in on the cheese-application stage, the girl would never learn to make a pizza properly. But more important, she would never WANT to learn. She would become sullen and insecure. She would run away from home and hop on a bus to LA. Then she would become addicted to heroin and fall in love with an abusive record label executive. All of that would happen if I kept her from cheesing the pizza. I swore to back off, to watch patiently and let her figure out things for herself. The cheese was in her hands now. She was in full control.

And God, she fucked it all up. I mean, it wasn't even close. There were slabs of cheese hanging over the sides. The spacing between slices was all uneven. She would jam the cheese into the dough and drag it around, creating huge snowbanks of red sauce and tearing holes—HOLES—in the crust. My pizza—my masterpizza—was being ruined in front of my eyes. It was like watching someone put his foot through a Van Gogh.

But I bit my lip. I had to. If I stepped in now . . . if I took away this precious learning opportunity, then all would be lost. I had to see this as a positive experience. My daughter would grow up strong and independent and it would all be thanks to my decision to let her make a pizza. A horrible, flavorless, overworked pizza. Surely one night of poor eating wasn't worth a lifetime of—

"Let me do the cheese. You go watch TV."

"YAY!"

I finished the pizza and put it in the oven. Twenty minutes later, it came out perfectly.

NICU

Before the malrotation, before the phone call from the operating room to let us know if our new son was going to live, there were the arguments for and against a third child. Having a third child means you should never again expect the world to sympathize with you. Even people with two kids deserve some compassion because until you have two children, you have no idea how big a pain in the ass two kids are. You think it's going to be double the work, but it's not. It's *four* times the work because you're managing both the kids *and* the complex relationship between them, which is exhausting. The burden grows exponentially. That's two children ruining your pizza instead of just one.

People with four or more kids are crazy people who belong in jail, but three edges between being dedicated to family and being a glutton for punishment. I was never 100 percent into the idea. While we were in the trying-to-conceive stage, my wife would tell me to get away from the microwave whenever I heated my leftovers so that my testicles wouldn't get bombarded with a dash of extra radiation. But sometimes, I would stand in front of it anyway.

"Get away from there!" she said once.

"Are you sure? Because, you know, we've got two nice kids. Tempting to quit while we're ahead, no?"

"I know. I know it's not the easiest decision. But seriously, stop cooking your balls."

So we knew three kids would be a world of shit going in. But after a while, we deluded ourselves into thinking it would be relatively easy. We were veterans of the birthing process. The wife would go to the hospital, get C-sectioned real good, and we'd be all set to go. That's one of the perks of having extra kids. You get to walk into that hospital acting like you own the place. You get to sneer at all the newbie parents who have no idea where the delivery ward is. There are no surprises waiting for you.

Except when your wife begins contracting at seven months and needs to be rushed to the hospital for early delivery. Except when they bring out fancy new high-resolution ultrasound machines that look ready to transform back into Optimus Prime at any moment, machines that end up detecting certain "abnormalities" in the fetus. Except when a team of doctors including an ob-gyn and a high-risk fetal specialist comes in to explain to you and your wife that your son might have some kind of genetic hiccup, and then the specialist proceeds to hop onto Wikipedia in front of you because she knows so little about the condition she thinks your son might have.

We were in the antepartum unit when they told us about the fetus. His head was too big. His tongue was too big. The openings to his kidneys were dilated. They feared that he might have a genetic defect classified as an overgrowth syndrome—a suite of conditions with possible symptoms that range from the benign (you have a big head) to the severe (you are mentally retarded).

The ob-gyn suggested we might want to hold off on tying my wife's tubes during the C-section in case anything happened to the child and we wanted to try to have another one to replace it. There was no warning for any of this. A new and far more difficult future was suddenly THERE, eating us up and spitting us back out.

"I know this is a lot to absorb," said the ob-gyn. "We're going to leave now so you two can talk about it in private."

When the doctors left, my wife burst into tears.

"I wasn't ready for that," she said.

"Neither was I." I knelt by the hospital bed and gripped her hand. "But this is not the end," I told her. "It's not. Don't think this is the end. There's so much more of this life and so much of it will be good, I promise you. There will still be graduations and Christmases and weddings and everything that's wonderful, everything that's so much better than this. I swear it."

"I saw his face on the ultrasound. He was beautiful."

"This is not the end." And I wanted to believe that. I

hoped that, through the hot tubs and giant amusement park mousetraps and late-night arrests, perhaps we were trained for this exact moment, that we had enough strength and love to make it through the birth, the interminable wait for test results, the surgery, and the phone call. *That* phone call.

The baby had survived so much up to that point. He was delivered seven weeks early, but he could breathe. His eyes and heart and kidneys were all functioning properly. At one point, a neonatologist who never removed her surgical mask told me that the baby's brain scan had come back negative. He wasn't going to be mentally handicapped. He would be able to talk and think and learn just like his brother and sister could. I wept tears of joy in front of the doctor. She patted my arm gently and scurried away.

The baby had served nine days in the NICU so far with little complaint. But now came this. Now came the disembowelment.

I took the phone from the receptionist, and as I put it to my ear, I had a split second to imagine what it would be like if the surgical assistant told me that the baby's digestive system was compromised. That the baby would die. And the vision seemed so possible that I felt as if it were now inevitable. I prepared myself to deal with it. *This was meant to be. He was meant to live this long and no longer, and I will not spend the rest of my life bitter. I will not pine for some imaginary little boy with perfectly arranged insides who has the ability to live for eighty years because that's not who this boy was. He was meant to be dead. Please, God, don't let him be meant to be dead.*

"Mr. Magary?"

"Yes."

"This is Dr. Holman from the OR. Dr. Staffen has had a chance to examine the bowels and they are one hundred percent healthy. Your son is going to be just fine."

I responded loudly so that my wife could overhear. "He's going to be okay?"

"Yes, the doctor will be out to talk with you once the procedure is finished."

"Oh, thank you. Thank you very much. So he's not gonna die, right? I just want to make double sure."

"He's going to be all right."

I gave the phone back to the receptionist, and my wife and I collapsed into each other, heaving long sobs. Before this, I never knew that joy and misery could merge into a single emotion, that you could cry for ten-minute stretches while feeling simultaneously overjoyed and horrified. But now I knew it firsthand: a whole new dimension to the human condition. Call it joyful sadness. Call it sad joyfulness. Call it *jadness*. Who knows. All I know is that I had a hard time differentiating between THANK GOD MY SON IS ALIVE and HOLY SHIT MY SON JUST HAD HIS INTESTINES TOSSED. There was no clear division in that moment. There was just the overwhelming happening of it all. Kathy the NICU nurse brought us back to another private room where we sat, dazed from emotional overload.

"We may have to go to church now," my wife said to me.

"Yeah, maybe."

"I mean, you know. He's gonna live."

"I know. I do like having Sunday mornings free, though."

"It would teach the other two a bit of gratitude."

"That it would. I'm still not sure I believe any of that God stuff, but yeah. I want to be more grateful. If not to God, then to . . . I dunno . . . life, I suppose."

Half an hour later, the surgeon came in and told us that the baby was hunky-dory and already back up in the NICU. All that was left was to bust him out of there and bring him home. I was certain it would be a cinch. We were already past the hard part. Getting a baby out of the NICU would be nothing. It's EASY, isn't it?

No matter how fortunate you are in life, if you have a child in the NICU, you will feel like God ripped you off. Every day, you walk into the NICU praying that your child will finally be healthy enough to go home. And as you make that walk, you pass by dozens of new parents strolling out of the postpartum unit with healthy, happy, full-term babies. I walked to the NICU every day to see our baby and I would see new fathers pushing their wives out of the elevators, holding flower bouquets and IT'S A BOY balloons, and I would fight with all my strength to not feel as if I had been cheated. I already had two perfectly healthy, wonderful children. I had already been treated to two moments when I was just like the ecstatic families strolling out of the hospital. And our third child had survived being gutted and cleaned like a fish. There was no reason for me to be bitter. At all.

But the feeling was there, no matter how hard I fought against it. The shift between the maternity ward waiting room—with boisterous families either waiting or celebrating—and the entrance to the NICU was too jarring not to affect me. The NICU entrance lay past the third-floor lobby, through a set of double doors and down a silent white hall to a modest reception area, with a tiny waiting room of its own that was perpetually empty. I would check in by showing the receptionist my wristband (which was growing more faded and crackled by the day; I worried constantly about it falling off) and then wash my hands thoroughly at one of the two sinks to the left of the receptionist's desk. You were allowed to bring covered drinks into the NICU but I never did because I was the exact kind of person that would trip and fall and spill a forty-two-ounce Coke Zero directly into a newborn's respirator.

All NICU entrants had to sterilize their hands at a special washing station to prevent infection. There was a bathroom right next door to the station and I used it every time I visited because I was so terribly nervous about finding out the baby's status that I always ended up having to take a giant shit. Then I would worry that it was inappropriate to take a shit in a NICU. I would wash my hands compulsively afterward but still worry that I hadn't gotten all of the filth off, that I was spreading fecal matter all over the place and giving every infant in the unit meningitis with my poopy hands.

The NICU was divided into sections based upon the severity of each infant's condition. The ones at the back were high-risk babies that needed careful monitoring, my son among the unfortunates. As I walked to the back of the unit, I could always see the other babies along the way. Some weighed as little as a single pound. It seemed unfathomable to me that anything that small could grow at all, that it could add fat and muscle and become something other than a tiny, helpless little creature. Some of the babies were housed in bassinets lined with foil that had heat lamps shining on them at all times, like burgers set out for pickup in a T.G.I. Friday's kitchen. Some were being rocked gently and fed by traumatized mothers still wearing their hospital gowns. You could hear the babies crying, some of them emitting a high-pitched "neuro-cry" that was a clear signal that their brains had been compromised.

I tried not to stare at the other children because it seemed like I was being intrusive, but I couldn't help it. I would see doctors and nurses talk to other parents in hushed tones and wonder what was wrong with their children. The majority of babies were housed in alcoves, with only a curtain surrounding them for privacy. A handful of babies got actual private rooms. I wondered if you got a room because your baby was certain to pass away. All of the joy and anticipation you could feel in the main waiting area of the maternity ward was missing here. Once inside the NICU, there was nothing but angst. You knew that every second in this place, someone was holding his or her breath. I wondered how many couples walked out of the NICU every year empty-handed.

After the baby's surgery, I walked back to his isolette with my wife so that I could stare at him. The entire incubator was covered with a fitted giraffe blanket, to give parents a sense that this was a warm and cute place, not the terrifying place we all knew it to be. There was a flap at the top of the blanket that I could unsnap and open to look down at the baby, as if I were staring at fish underneath a glass bottom boat. I pulled the flap open and saw my son lying on a bili-blanket, a blanket that lit up with changing colors to help lower the baby's bilirubin levels (high levels of bilirubin cause jaundice). It would shift from green to yellow to red every few moments, as if my son were onstage at a rock concert.

"Should we take a picture of him?" I asked my wife.

She shook her head and began to cry. "I don't want to remember any of this."

There were tubes and wires sprouting out from all over his body. There were three wires running from his foot that went directly to a monitor that displayed his heart rate, his blood pressure, and the oxygen levels in his blood. Whenever the vitals got too high or too low, the monitor would beep like a smoke alarm and the nurses would come over to make sure the child wasn't dying. Sometimes a baby will forget to breathe and his heart rate will plunge down to virtually nothing before the nurse gives him a nudge and he suddenly remembers, "Oh, hey! OXYGEN." This is called bradycardia, or a "brady" for short. Our son bradyed a lot. It was fucking scary as hell.

All over the NICU, something was always beeping. If not our son's monitor, then someone else's IV. The nurses would rush to another alcove and I would find myself grateful there was a baby sicker than my own. I hated myself for thinking that. I had a hard time recognizing which beep was coming from where. Every beep was a chance to worry. The beeps rained down twenty-four hours a day, from all directions. The nurses had clearly gotten used to them. I never did. A handful of unlucky parents had to take the monitors home with them when their children were discharged, to keep tabs on their vital signs. Those home monitors often malfunctioned, beeping all night long.

For days after surgery, the baby's stomach needed to be completely empty. The nurses placed a tube in his mouth that snaked all the way down to the inner lining of his stomach, to suck up all the excess fluids. Once we began feeding him, we would have to make sure that no nasty green fluid came back up. Otherwise it would be back to the OR, and without any guarantee that things would turn out okay a second time.

There was also a CPAP device, a cumbersome series of nasal tubes that made it look like the baby had a snorkel pasted to his nose. The tubes ran to a pump that periodically blasted air into the baby's lungs because, although his lungs were functional, he didn't yet have the strength to take in enough oxygen on his own. The tubes had to be held in place with clear plastic tape, and I could see the tape pulling at my son's cheeks, dragging them up with the tube and giving him a deranged Joker smile that I didn't want him to have. There was an IV running from a prick in his heel that delivered vital nutrients straight into his bloodstream since he wasn't allowed to take food orally yet, plus fentanyl to keep the pain away. The IV was held fast in place by surgical tape that wrapped around his foot again and again, like a little mummy foot. I could see his toes turning red from all the capillaries being squeezed together.

There were two hard plastic flaps on either side of the isolette that swung open so that we could touch the baby, like nuclear plant workers carefully handling plutonium. One night, I stared down through the top panel and I saw my own hand reaching in to gently pat his chest. Then I kissed the plastic roof of the isolette as if it were an outer layer of his own skin. I whispered to him, "This is the only time you get to break my heart."

I cried and I could see the tears dripping down onto the plastic, obscuring my view. That's all you can do when your baby is in the NICU. You cry and you cry and you don't stop crying until the child is finally home. You don't even realize you can cry that much. I would cry low and soft, just a little "Ohhhhhhh . . . ," the tears soaking my collar. I cried as if I had just broken something that I'd never be able to fix. Eventually, the crying became a nuisance, a hindrance to my wife and me being fully functional and able to solve problems like grown adults. I just wanted him to be home. I knew he had to be in the NICU for a long time— weeks, months, perhaps even half a year. He would die otherwise. Still, I wanted him out of this horrible place. If I could just get him home to his crib, to his mother and brother and sister, then everything would be fine. I knew it.

The isolette itself was a remarkable piece of machinery. It had a retractable roof, like a new stadium. And it had little foot pedals so you could make the entire thing go up and down and up and down, which was good because sometimes

I had to stoop to reach through the flaps and then my back would hurt and then I'd feel like an asshole for worrying about my back when my kid was in intensive care. A few days after the surgery, I visited the baby on my own late at night after work while my wife rested at home. I pressed a button on the isolette out of curiosity and the roof came off, sounding an alarm and causing a nurse to sprint over to close it back up.

"You can't open it," she said.

"Holy shit, I'm so sorry," I said. "Did I kill him?"

"No, no, he'll be fine. But the roof needs to stay closed so that we can control the temperature of the air around him."

"So this thing has air-conditioning?"

"And heat. It's the Mercedes of isolettes."

I immediately wondered what the Mercedes of isolettes cost, and how that cost would then be passed on to me, Mr. Health Care Consumer. I tried to avoid thinking about money while the child was in the NICU, but it was difficult with new thick envelopes from the insurance company arriving every day, listing out very large numbers that scared the piss out of me. Part of me wanted to get my son home just so that the paperwork would stop piling up. I thought about what the final tally would be. Millions? Billions? Trillions? They could have presented me with any figure and I wouldn't have been shocked.

"I'm going to need you to sign a consent form," the nurse told me.

"For what?"

"Dr. Earvin says that your son needs a minor blood transfusion."

"Is that normal?" That's what I asked the nurse or doctor every time something insane happened with our new child. *Oh, he needs intestinal surgery and a blood transfusion? That's normal, right?* I needed constant reassurance that all of this was routine, that somehow my son wasn't the only one to suffer through this particular gauntlet of conditions.

"I mean, it's not *normal* normal, but it's perfectly safe."

"He's not gonna get the infected blood, is he?" I worried that I would sign the form and there would be no clean blood, and they would have to give my son the filthy, herpes-ridden backup blood instead.

"No, no. The blood we use in the NICU is the cleanest blood possible. It's way cleaner than the blood we give adults."

"Holy shit, don't tell me that." I pictured a bag of donated adult blood with eight used Band-Aids floating around inside it.

"Rest assured, the blood we give him is sterilized to the nth degree."

I signed the form.

"Do you want to do Kangaroo Care?" the nurse asked. Kangaroo Care is when you hold a shirtless preemie against your bare chest. The skin-on-skin contact calms both the parent and the child.

"Sure," I said.

She wheeled in a hospital-issued recliner with cheap vinyl upholstery and drew the curtain around the alcove. I unbuttoned my shirt and sat down, maneuvering the recliner as close to the isolette as possible. She raised the roof of the isolette and flipped down the side, then carefully gathered up all the wires so that none of them would snag. She unswaddled the baby so his warm bare skin could press up against mine. I could see the smear of dried surgical glue holding the two-inch incision on his belly together. She handed him to me and I kicked back with him nestled in my chest hair. It was like holding my heart in my own hands. I wanted to cut open my chest and hide him in my blood, where nothing could touch him. I felt the same way I did back when I was in eighth grade and I was in love with this one girl who didn't love me back. My heart ached the exact same way, though I don't know why. I kissed his hairy little head and began to sing to him.

> Baa, baa, Black Sheep, have you any wool?
> Yes, sir, yes, sir, three bags full.
> One for my master and one for my dame
> And one for the little boy who lives down the lane.
> Baa, baa, Black Sheep, have you any wool?
> Yes, sir, yes, sir, three bags full.

The NICU didn't allow such tender private moments to go on for very long. The families in the NICU were all packed together, and the alcove curtain offered only the illusion of having your own room. On the other side of the curtain was another parent, a mother tending to her infant. I could hear the other mother singing to her baby too: a low repetitive drone that I thought was lacking in creativity. I sang a little bit louder to drown her out, but then she sang louder, and now we were trying to upstage each other like we were the Supremes. Eventually, I relented and stopped singing, holding the baby close and pretending that we were the only people in the NICU, the world, the universe. Just us.

"I'm gonna get you out of here," I whispered to him. "I'm gonna get you out of here and when I do, you will see everything. There's so much more out there waiting for you. You have no fucking idea."

I drove home that night and passed by a car fire on the side of the highway. The flames engulfed the entire vehicle, like something out of a cheap Mob film, and rose up to three times the car's original height. I always tried to mentally rank the car accidents I passed by on the road, trying to remember if I'd ever seen a worse accident. I gave bonus points for the sight of a gurney. I had never seen an accident like that before. Ever.

There is a list of benchmarks that a baby has to meet in order to be discharged from a NICU. It has to weigh a certain amount. It has to be able to breathe on its own. It needs to maintain a steady body temperature. It has to stop bradying for a full twenty-four to forty-eight hours. And it needs to be able to take food by mouth without emesis. The progress it makes toward hitting these benchmarks is not a straight upward trajectory. Preemies can make progress, and then regress, and then get back to where they were, and then regress even further back. Every time there's a regression, you feel utterly demoralized, as if you can't stand it any longer. Our son was eventually cleared to eat several times, only to throw everything back up and go back to relying exclusively on IV nutrients.

Every morning I would wake up and call the NICU to check on the baby's progress during the night. *Was he alive? Did he have any bradys? Was he able to eat? Did he shit? How big of a shit was it? TELL ME, TELL ME, TELL ME.* The nurses changed shifts at seven thirty in the morning and I would always ask who the new nurse on duty was, praying the baby would get one we liked. When the baby had a nurse we liked, we would hold out hope that the nurse would decide to work a 128-hour shift. We hit for the cycle with the NICU ward nurses. We managed to get every single one of them. Most of them we liked; some of them we didn't. All of them admirably performed a job that I myself couldn't possibly stomach. Sometimes I wondered how many babies died on a nurse's watch each week. What happens when you have to stagger home after witnessing that, after watching devastated parents wail their souls out?

I came in one night to visit the baby (I often went to the hospital alone after work; my wife would stay with the other two kids after being at the hospital all day). They had placed the suction tube back in his mouth, so I checked in the receptacle under the isolette that was used to collect anything that had been sucked out of the baby's stomach. I saw greenish fluid in the container and immediately began to freak out. I checked the baby's nose and there was dried snot caked all over the CPAP. He had been drooling and little crystals had formed around his mouth near the tube. It made him look neglected and I became silently pissed at the nurses for neglecting him, which was actually a cheap way of covering up my own guilt for not being at the baby's side every waking second—for leaving him here in this place, so alone and helpless.

There was no nurse nearby and I grew white with anxiety. *The fluid is green and now he has to be split open again and maybe he'll die this time and we've come too far for this to end this way now please.* The curtain to the alcove was open and there was no giraffe blanket covering the isolette. I felt like my son had been left naked out in the open to rot under the fluorescent lights. I pulled the curtain and put the blanket back over him, trying to close the space between the flaps so that the lights couldn't get to him—the horrible, horrible lights. I dabbled at his face with a wet cloth to clean the snot and drool away. I scoured the unit with my eyes, desperate to find a nurse to make stern eye contact with. I heard strange voices coming from the isolette next door and I realized that the baby in that isolette was a new arrival. I could hear a nurse talking to the mother . . .

"Are you going to pump while you're in rehab?"
Holy shit.
"We have to keep her on methadone for now, to wean her off the heroin because that was still in her bloodstream."
HOLY FUCKITY FUCK.

I peered around the curtain to get a look and saw a sixteen-year-old girl in a hospital gown. It wasn't her first child. The nurse sensed my presence and gave me a firm "I'll be right with you." But she wasn't. Minutes passed and

I grew pissed off at the white trash heroin addict next door who was siphoning away precious nursing time from my own child. Meanwhile, I could hear the poor heroin baby screaming, and I felt a keen sense of dread for the life that awaited her. Outside of this NICU, things would get no better.

I reached into the isolette and rubbed my son's tummy. Every second that I spent waiting for the nurse grew more pronounced. When she had given her final warning to the mom next door to stop using heroin, she came to see me and I poured out all my worries.

"There's green stuff in his container and his face was dirty and the CPAP doesn't look right on him."

"Sir, sir. It's okay. That greenish fluid is just residue from prior to the surgery. If it were greener, we'd be alarmed. But this older kind of residue is completely expected."

"So he's not going to need another surgery?"

"No. He's actually had a great night so far. You can try to feed him again."

I started to cry. "I'm just so scared, I just saw that green stuff and, God, I just want him to be okay, you know?" Then she put her arm around me and I didn't feel so alone. I had a blanket from the baby's isolette that I had nicked from the ward to bring home so that I could catch his scent whenever I slept at night, whenever he wasn't close by. But the blanket had begun to lose his scent, so I swapped it out for another one in his isolette that had more of him embedded in its fabric. The nurse pulled the baby out and checked his weight and his vitals while I dutifully texted his progress to my wife and my mother and my sister and brother.

They took him off the CPAP respirator and gave him a cannula, one of those little plastic nostril tubes you see on old folks who wheel around oxygen tanks. The night had turned. His lungs were getting stronger. I texted the news to my wife excitedly, as if the baby had struck oil. I got home that night and debriefed my wife on what I'd seen.

"The mom next to us is a heroin addict."

She sat straight up in bed. "WHAT?!"

"Calm down, calm down. I mean, it's not like the mom is gonna stab our child with a used needle." Though now that I mentioned it, I couldn't stop picturing it happening.

"Is the baby addicted to heroin too?"

"Yes."

She began to cry. "That's so sad. It's just a little baby."

"I know." I put my arm around her and she cried some more.

At one point, my parents came to visit the baby. I put on a brave face, telling them that their new grandson would get out of the NICU any day now, when I didn't really have any clue. One afternoon, I was in the kitchen and couldn't keep up the facade. I broke down in tears with my father in the next room over. I think I wanted him to hear me. I didn't bother trying to hide my distress. He took his cue, walked into the kitchen, and, without saying anything, wrapped me up in his arms. He was wearing this big leather jacket and I burrowed into it like a three-year-old. For a minute, it was nice to be more of a son than a father.

The baby still wasn't eating enough. We kept trying to feed him orally but he'd swiftly throw it all back up. They ran a feeding tube up his nose and down to his stomach to help supplement the oral feedings. Sometimes there was blood in his spit-up because the feeding tube would irritate his digestive lining. We would try to feed him again a day later— trying out bigger nipples and crosscut nipples to see if that helped—and still get the same result. Every text my wife and I exchanged became a simple inventory of how many cubic centimeters of fluid the child had taken by mouth that day. Five. Ten. Zero. The number he needed to hit to get out of the NICU was fifty. It seemed eons away.

To supplement both the feeding tube and the attempted oral feedings, he was still getting some nutrients intrave-nously: lipids and proteins and sugars. But now the nurses were struggling to find usable veins to tap. Like a heroin addict, a baby in a NICU soon runs out of suitable entry points for a needle. Our son had now exhausted virtually every spot on his arms, hands, legs, and feet. I was in the hospital one night when the final viable tapping point came loose.

"Oops," said the nurse. "His IV came out again."

"Can you find another?" I asked.

"I can try, but you might want to leave the room for it."

"No. No, I'll stay here with him."

I deeply regretted it. I took his hand as the nurse

swabbed his tiny little foot and dug the needle in, trying to break through an all-important vein wall. He shrieked for help, confused as to why all this was happening, why he had to endure the lights and the beeps and the needles. I felt as if I were the one stabbing him, as if I were the one inflicting that horrible, unexplained pain upon him. I held his hand but didn't feel like I had earned the right. I had betrayed him. I had made him suffer through this. Eventually, the nurse backed off.

"What now?" I asked.

"We may have to go through his scalp."

She brought in one of the neonatologists on call and I overheard them deliberating. They were going to shave a portion of his scalp and tap a line there: a PICC line—a special, long-term IV with a catheter that runs all the way down the vein to the entrance of the infant's beating heart. I heard them deliberating and pictured the baby being held down and sheared like a lamb. *NONONONONONO*. I walked up to the nurse and the doctor, knowing full well that I had little chance of overruling them.

"Can I just talk to both of you before we go ahead with this, before I sign my consent?"

The doctor raised her eyes. "Okay."

"Please don't do this," I begged. "Please. I can't let this happen to him. I can't let you shave his head and poke holes in it. Give him a chance to eat his way out of this. He can do it. I know he can."

"You understand that with preemies, it's not so cut-and-dried, right?"

"I know that. All I'm asking is that you give him a chance."

She sighed. "Okay, he's got twenty-four hours. If he can't hold his food down by then, we'll have to reevaluate."

"Thank you. Thank you so, so much. You won't regret this."

I watched as the nurse took away the nasty IV equipment that had remained by his bedside at all times. One wire was gone. I wasn't going to let him regress. I was well aware that he *could* regress, and I warned myself to be emotionally prepared for it. But fuck that. He was gonna eat. He was gonna eat like a fucking champ.

I sat down in the vinyl recliner as the nurse laid him in my lap and I took the hospital-issued bottle with twenty CCs of formula and began to feed him. The nurse stepped away and I turned into a deranged cheerleader.

"Come on, son. COME ON. You can do this."

The baby sucked and sucked and the progress was painstaking. I paused to burp him every few minutes and it seemed as if he had barely made a dent.

"Don't stop now, boy. If you wanna get out of here, you gotta eat."

After a few minutes, he got into a rhythm, slurping down more and more.

"That's it! You're doing it!"

By the end, he had sucked down a mighty eighteen CCs. I stared at the bottle and thought about what to do with the two CCs remaining. *Maybe I should drink it.* I stood up with the baby and he spit up all over the hospital floor, but no one apart from me had noticed. Quick as I could, I set him back in the isolette, mopped up the mess, and washed out the bottle. By the time the nurse came back, my tracks were covered.

"How'd he do?" she asked.

"Twenty CCs. No barf!"

"That's great!"

I texted my wife that I managed to get the IV out and she texted back, "SHUT UP. HOW'D YOU DO THAT?" I exalted in working my magic. I had never won an argument with a doctor before in my life. It made me feel like a goddamn superhero.

Over the next few days, the barfing went down. The baby began to take all his bottles for real, without me doctoring the evidence. Twenty CCs became thirty. Thirty became forty. Forty became forty-two, then forty-three, then *holy shit, get to fifty already, kid*. Every time he hit a new feeding plateau, I walked out of the NICU pumping my fist, screaming out "FUCK YEAH!" at the top of my lungs if no one was around. They removed the cannula from his nose, leaving him free to breathe on his own. Outside the NICU, in the lonely white hall leading back to the reception area, there was a series of photographs of the hospital's annual NICU reunions: hundreds of happy parents with now-healthy babies waving gaily to the camera, having forgotten all about their time inside the hospital walls. I wanted to go there. I wanted to get to THAT. Now we were close. *You're doing it, boy. Don't stop fighting.*

• • •

We came in one morning and they had moved the baby over to a lower-risk part of the NICU, a section for babies who would be going home sooner rather than later. He was out of the isolette now, lying in a simple plastic tub bassinet. The night nurse had written our son's name out on a green index card and taped it to the side of the tub and when I saw it I started to cry. I remembered the moment he was born in the operating room, hearing him cry and knowing he wasn't going to be stillborn. The attending nurse that day asked me his name, and when I said the name out loud his name became a promise—a blood oath to dedicate the rest of my life to keeping him alive and happy. Now he was here, on the verge of being discharged. Alive. Happy.

My wife sat with him in the recliner and fed him fifty CCs straight, no chaser. The feeding tube was gone. A day later, we watched the nurse unhook him from the heart rate monitor and now he was free, 100 percent wireless. No more IVs. No more heel pricks. No more nurses. He was just a baby now, not unlike any other.

For his discharge day, we brought along our other two kids, who had visited the NICU on occasion only to end up pushing all the buttons and demanding to go to the cafeteria for chicken fingers. I pictured our walk out of the NICU as something wonderfully poignant. I had the final movie reel playing in my head. Everyone would get along for the baby's sake and we would stroll out of the hospital as a loving family unit.

But then the two older kids fought over who got to strap the baby in.

"I WANNA DO IT!" my daughter screamed.

"NO, I WANNOO!" said the boy.

"Listen," I said. "There are other babies here and they're trying to sleep because this place sucks. Besides, this baby is very delicate and I don't want either of you killing him by accident. I will let you screw up everything else today, including the pizza."

"NO!" they replied in unison.

"Oh god dammit."

My wife pulled out a camera. "Let's try to get a picture."

I held the camera out and snapped an attempted Christmas card photo while we crowded around the baby carrier and the two older children jockeyed for a position closest to the baby's head.

"Will you two get away from his head? It's got soft spots!" I said.

"Drew," my wife said, "keep it down."

"I'm sorry, I'm sorry. This isn't how I pictured this moment."

"It's never gonna be perfect. Let's just go home."

So we did. After twenty-seven days in the hospital, our son finally came home.

A few weeks later, I was drinking wine after dinner (no driving!) and walking around with the baby strapped to my body in a Björn. I loved having the baby in the Björn because I could pretend there was an alien popping out of my stomach. The girl and I had discovered that the baby liked really loud music. At least, I think the baby liked it. If he didn't like it, at least the music drowned out his protests. She ran up to my computer and demanded I put on the loudest shit possible.

"The baby wants to hear the music!" she screamed.

So I cranked it up and started dancing around, the baby's arms and legs swinging freely in the air. The boy came into the room and started hopping around.

"Is that your pee-pee dance?" I asked him.

"No, I'm just dancing, Deddy!"

"Are you sure?"

"Wes! I wannoo dance too!"

"That music's a little loud, isn't it?" my wife asked.

"Nonsense," I said. "Look at the baby. He loves it."

"I can't see his face because it's buried in your chest."

"You're just gonna have to take my word for it. RAWK!"

My daughter ran up to the boy and hugged him.

"Whoa, hey, that's not one of those evil hugs, is it?" I asked.

"No! I'm just hugging him. See?"

"Oh. Oh, carry on, then."

We all started to rock, and I leaned into the baby and whispered in his ear, "I'm glad you're here, son. I'm so glad you're here."

I wish I could tell you that everything that came after this little scene was blissful, but of course it wasn't. There were still arguments and brothers shoving sisters and sisters shoving brothers, and more heartache and more worry and more everything. All the bullshit you sign up for when you start out doesn't just go away. It goes on and on and on until you stop running away from it and start embracing it, until you realize that all the trips to the grocery store, all the nervous fretting at the playground, all the terrifying trips to the doctor are what truly *matter*. It becomes your reason for living, the thing that means more to your life than your life itself. It's never gonna be perfect—no, it's not. You're gonna keep fucking up, and fucking up badly. But you can't give up. You have to keep fighting to make things right. Because that's what love is. Love means you never stop trying to be better.

ACKNOWLEDGMENTS

There's a certain deliberate thoughtlessness that goes into writing about your family. You have to be willing to expose things they may or may not want exposed, to potentially mortify them all for the sake of entertaining a bunch of strangers. This is especially true in the case of my children, who are still far too young to grab me by the shirt collar and be like, "Hey, Dad, IX-NAY ON THE PEEING IN THE OTTUB-HAY." So I'd like to thank my family for their unending love and patience. You kids get an extra hour of TV as reparations. Pretty sweet deal, if you ask me.

I'm also indebted to my parents and my wife's parents for their love and support and for all their free babysitting, because babysitting rates these days are complete bullshit. Seriously, fifteen bucks an hour? I didn't see you build me a coffee table while we were out to dinner.

ACKNOWLEDGMENTS

Professionally, I am again forever indebted to Byrd Leavell of the Waxman Leavell Agency for helping me see this project through. There are so many agents out there who don't give a shit, but Byrd has never had a problem making time to answer my pointless emails and help me work through any sort of structural problem I have writing a book, making sure that book represents one clean, simple idea. If you're a young writer and you have the fortune of getting a call from Byrd, hire that man. Hire that man and extract all the free drinks out of him that you can. He's the bestest.

I'm also grateful to Patrick Mulligan and Lauren Marino at Gotham for their judicious editing, along with production editor Erica Ferguson, copy editor Mary Beth Constant, proofreaders Rick Ball and Anne Heausler, designer Spring Hoteling, production supervisor Bob Wojciechowski, publicity manager Anne Kosmoski, editorial assistant Emily Wunderlich, and the art team of Monica Benalcazar and Stephen Brayda, who created a brilliant cover. It was incumbent upon me to write something that lived up to that cover, and I hope I did.

There were a handful of friends and colleagues who gave me advice and/or support during the writing of this book, and I'd like to thank them all, including my wife, Howard Spector, Jesse Johnston, Spencer Hall, Justin Halpern, Will Leitch, Matt Ufford, Jack Kogod, Peter de Saint Phalle, and more. I owe a big thanks to Tommy Craggs and AJ Daulerio for championing me to the powers that be at Gawker, and to Scott Kidder and Nick Denton for bringing me on board full time. I'm also grateful to Jim Nelson and Devin Gordon at *GQ* for taking me in and giving me access to their secret vault of man-scarves and steampunk apparel.

Finally, my youngest son would not be alive today without the care of all the doctors and nurses at Shady Grove Adventist Hospital in Gaithersburg, Maryland. I will never stop being grateful to them. I feel like a smaller man when I consider the amount of skill and mental fortitude they need to do their jobs every day. I couldn't do that. That's real work. I remain forever in awe of all of you. Thank you for saving our boy.